WHITE SPACES IN SHAKESPEARE

White Spaces
In Shakespeare

The Development of the Modern Text

Paul Bertram

BELLFLOWER PRESS

Case Western Reserve University
Cleveland, Ohio

Copyright © 1981 by Bellflower Press
Department of English
Case Western Reserve University
Cleveland, Ohio 44106

Grateful acknowledgment is made to the Rare Book Division, The New York Public Library, Astor, Lenox and Tilden Foundations, for permission to reproduce portions of pp. 352-353 of *Mr. William Shakespeares Comedies, Histories, & Tragedies*, London, 1623.

The publication of this book has been made possible by the generosity of W. Powell Jones, Aaron Jacobson, and the University Research Council of Rutgers University.

Library of Congress Cataloging in Publication Data

Bertram, Paul Benjamin.
　White spaces in Shakespeare.

　　Bibliography: pp. 79-85.
　　Includes index.
　　1. Shakespeare, William, 1564-1616—Criticism, Textual. 2. Shakespeare, William, 1564-1616—Versification. I. Title.
PR3071.B4 1981　　822.3'3　81-1713
　　　　　　　AACR2

ISBN: 0-934958-01-7 (hardbound)
ISBN: 0-934958-02-5 (paperbound)

Manufactured in the United States of America

Contents

Foreword, by Maynard Mack   vii

Preface   ix

White Spaces in Shakespeare   3

Afterword   69

Bibliography   79

Index   86

Foreword

What feature of great literary importance distinguishes the second from the first issue of the Third Folio? If the Quartos of *Romeo and Juliet* had been lost, where would you turn to find a text of its Prologue? Presented with a 1608 Quarto of *King Lear* in your favorite research library, why should you ask to see the librarian?

If you have answered these questions correctly, *White Spaces in Shakespeare* is still a book for you. It is a book for everyone who reads, directs, teaches, acts in, writes about or goes to see Shakespeare's plays. Admirably lucid, mercifully succinct, it offers the best overview I know of the long road (white with the bleaching bones of editorial Ozymandiases) that runs from the Quartos and First Folio to the best texts extant in 1980.

Moreover, it points beyond. For a point that Professor Bertram rightly stresses is that while we have left no stone unturned to achieve a text close to what Shakespeare wrote, we have been shockingly neglectful of how Shakespeare intended that text to be spoken. On this, the lineation of the First Folio in particular affords a world of hints, most of which even respected modern textualists ignore, preferring (to give but one instance) the reconstituted plastic of the following:

> You are dull, Casca, and those sparks of life
> That should be in a Roman you do want,
> Or else you use not. You look pale, and gaze,

And put on fear, and cast yourself in wonder —

to the same lines as they actually appear in the First Folio, "swarming" (to borrow Professor Bertram's words) "with vital clues to pauses and emphasis, a storehouse of acting information on the sound and weight and feel of the voices":

> You are dull, Casca,
> And those sparks of life, that should be in a Roman,
> You do want, or else you use not.
> You look pale, and gaze, and put on fear,
> And cast yourself in wonder . . .

But this is not the place to recapitulate Professor Bertram's compelling argument. Suffice it to say that all you who edit Shakespeare in time to come should digest it carefully and then set out to repair the error of your forefathers.

Huntington Library   Maynard Mack
1 July 1980

Preface

White Spaces in Shakespeare offers a fresh perspective on the historical progress of editors and other scholars in determining the authentic text of Shakespeare. Presented as a capsule history of Shakespeare's text from the 1590's to the 1970's (and presuming no prior special knowledge of the subject), it is also designed to show how certain radical and widespread revisions in Shakespeare's verse and prose, invented by his earliest editors in the eighteenth century, have been uncritically perpetuated in almost all editions down to our own day.

The essay aims at bringing the entire textual history of Shakespeare within a single critical scope, brief enough to be taken in at a single reading. It identifies all the major innovations and discoveries that have contributed over the centuries to the development of the modern received text, while at the same time it points up the re-use in that text of neo-classical metrical revisions that distort or obscure many of the original spoken rhythms (for which the early quarto and Folio textual sources are the only authorities). In this respect it is both a short history of Shakespeare's text, making clear the circumstances in which key textual changes have come about, and a basic reexamination of current textual premises, pointing the way toward new editions of the plays that would be notably superior to present ones in their approach to authenticity.

For their interest, encouragement, criticism, and other assistance, consciously and unconsciously given, I am deeply indebted to Sydell Carlton, Maurice Charney, Thomas R. Edwards, Paul Fussell, Daniel A. Howard, Francis A. Johns, George Kearns, Bridget Gellert Lyons, C. F. Main, Maynard Mack, Richard Poirier, Robert Rockman, and William H. Youngren. For generous support that made it possible to carry out this project I am grateful to the University Research Council, and to the Faculty Academic Study Program, both of Rutgers University.

P. B.

New Brunswick, New Jersey

White Spaces
In Shakespeare

White Spaces in Shakespeare

> What the public is here to expect is a true and correct edition of Shakespeare's works, cleared from the corruptions with which they have hitherto abounded.
>
> Sir Thomas Hanmer, 1744

No fewer than sixty separate editions of poems and plays by Shakespeare were printed and sold during his lifetime, but virtually all of them remained unknown to his earliest modern editor (Nicholas Rowe) in 1709. The outlook of editors has been enlarged many times over since then, and as a result the distance between the public and "a true and correct edition" has been many times foreshortened. The best editions of the present day, for example, generally surpass in accuracy the standard text of Victorian times, the Cambridge-Globe Shakespeare (1864), to the extent of thousands of particular readings — quite as wide a margin as that by which the Cambridge-Globe edition surpasses those of the editorial pioneers. The pages that follow (beginning with a thumbnail sketch of the early editions) take up a few episodes in editorial history as they reflect progressively changing conceptions, both metrical and verbal, of the received text.

The text of the earliest Shakespeare editions to reach the book market, *Venus and Adonis* (1593) and *The Rape of Lucrece* (1594), could hardly have been more "true and correct," since both publications had been initiated and were evidently proofread by the author. On the other hand the play texts that arrived at the printing house had to travel through the more roundabout routes of the theatrical profession. In some cases a stationer might publish a popular play from a manuscript that had been abridged, either legitimately or by some unauthorized means, for provincial performance. Or, at the other extreme, he might be provided by Shakespeare's company with a complete manuscript in Shakespeare's hand (possibly bearing annotations by the company prompt-book keeper) — in a few cases because the company may have wanted to replace an earlier corrupt edition whose original publication they had not been able to prevent. In either case the publishers' selling points on the title pages of the early editions were the descriptive titles of the plays[1] and sometimes the names of the acting companies,[2] but not, in any of the editions extant from 1597 or before, the name of the author. By 1598, however, Shakespeare's name had been added to reprint editions of *Richard II* and *Richard III* and began to appear commonly among the other essential advertising notices on title pages — even at times

1. Such as *The First Part of the Contention betwixt the two famous Houses of York and Lancaster, with the death of the good Duke Humphrey: And the banishment and death of the Duke of Suffolk, and the Tragical end of the proud Cardinal of Winchester, with the notable Rebellion of Jack Cade: And the Duke of York's first claim unto the Crown* (1594), an abridgment of the play that the 1623 Folio titles *The Second Part of Henry the Sixth, with the death of the Good Duke Humphrey.*

2. *The Most Lamentable Roman Tragedy of Titus Andronicus. As it was played by the Right Honourable the Earl of Derby, Earl of Pembroke, and Earl of Sussex their Servants* (1594); to these names the 1600 reprint adds that of the Chamberlain's Men.

on plays like *The London Prodigal* (1605) and *A Yorkshire Tragedy* (1608) that he did not write. In 1622 the stationer who brought out the first edition of *Othello* could say in a preface, "To commend it, I will not, . . . because the author's name is sufficient to vent his work."

In 1616 the first collected edition of Ben Jonson's *Works,* a folio volume of over a thousand pages, set the precedent for publishing English plays in something more durable than sixpenny pamphlets. The King's Men (whose senior partners were then Richard Burbage, John Hemmings, and Henry Condell, the three London friends to whom Shakespeare bequeathed memorial rings) continued to perform Shakespeare's plays at their two theaters. Before anyone in the company took steps to arrange for their publication, however, the bookseller Thomas Pavier undertook a project of his own (devious enough to remain concealed for three centuries) to supply the reading market with a Shakespeare collection. Pavier owned or acquired, properly (that is, within the rules of the Stationers' Company governing the book trade), the printing rights to ten plays that had last been published between 1600 and 1611; he reprinted them all in 1619 (sometimes adding fresh ascriptions to Shakespeare) and marketed them together. In May of the same year the Stationers' Company received a directive from the Lord Chamberlain forbidding the publication of plays owned by the King's Men without their consent. Pavier proceeded anyway, imperfectly covering his traces by the use of fake publishing imprints and false dates on several of the plays. (Early in the twentieth century Alfred Pollard was surprised to encounter more than one instance of a bound volume in which the same ten editions, showing the identical pattern of miscellaneous dates, had apparently been brought together. This coincidence led to further investigation, especially into the physical evidence of type-ornaments and watermarks, which proved that all ten editions in question, including five that were dated either 1600 or 1608, had in fact been produced in the same shop in 1619.) This so-called Collection of 1619 included reprints of two plays not by Shakespeare and of four others derived from badly abridged editions. (The publishing lines, with the misdated items shown in their proper place, may be seen in the table of editions to 1619, pages 8-9.) The disclosure of the Pavier enterprise, besides helping to set into sharper relief the different kind of publishing venture that Hemmings and Condell carried out afterwards, removed obstacles that had served to distort the perspective of Shakespeare editors for two centuries.

The copy for thirty-six plays proceeded through William Jaggard's printing house into the 1623 Folio. Hemmings and Condell supplied manuscripts for the eighteen plays being published for the first time[3] and made available complete versions of four plays that had been previously published only in radically abridged versions.[4] The texts of the remaining fourteen plays diverge relatively little from the previously published editions in eight cases,[5] more

---

3. *The Tempest, Two Gentlemen of Verona, Measure for Measure, The Comedy of Errors, As You Like It, All's Well that Ends Well, Twelfth Night, The Winter's Tale, Henry VI Part 1, Henry VIII, Coriolanus, Timon of Athens, Julius Caesar, Macbeth, Antony and Cleopatra, Cymbeline; King John, The Taming of the Shrew.*

4. *Henry VI Part 2* (3353 lines in F, 2213 in Q), *Henry VI Part 3* (3217/2311), *Henry V* (3376/1721), *Merry Wives of Windsor* (2701/1620). (As indicated in the table, analogous abridgments in the first editions of *Romeo and Juliet* and *Hamlet* had already been replaced by authoritative texts in later quartos.)

widely in six,[6] and are now thought to have been set in most cases from printed quartos to which manuscript corrections had been added and in a few others from different manuscripts. Although the Folio did not contain all the plays that are now usually included in collected editions of Shakespeare,[7] it is the exclusive textual authority for eighteen plays and of crucial importance either in establishing or correcting the text of nearly all the others. For the plays that had been published before from different manuscripts, however, attention to their textual divergences would not be publicly drawn until the following century.

With the deaths of Hemmings and Condell, the responsibility for handling Shakespeare's text returned to the book trade. The First Folio, priced at £1 in a press run estimated to have been 1200 copies, sold well enough to warrant a reprint in less than nine years. The Second Folio (1632) was a reprint of the First; although it contains a sizable number of textual corrections (about two per page), along with routine modernizations of typography and spelling, none of them requires the assumption that any manuscripts had been freshly consulted. Its publisher, Thomas Cotes, had acquired the printing rights and other assets of the Jaggard firm, but

5. *Romeo and Juliet, Love's Labour's Lost, Henry IV Part 1, Much Ado about Nothing, A Midsummer Night's Dream, The Merchant of Venice, Titus Andronicus, Richard II.*

6. *Richard III, King Lear, Troilus and Cressida, Hamlet, Henry IV Part 2, Othello.*

7. *Pericles* was not included, nor was *The Two Noble Kinsmen* (first published in 1634 with a title-page ascription to Shakespeare and John Fletcher). Editors today usually include also the episodes Shakespeare contributed to a thirty-ninth play, *Sir Thomas More* (first published in 1844).

Shakespearean (and pseudo-Shakespearean) editions to 1619:

	Henry VI Part 2	Henry VI Part 3	Richard III	Titus Andronicus	Romeo and Juliet	Love's Labour's Lost	Richard II	Mids. Night's Dream	Henry IV Part 1	Merchant of Venice
1594	[Q1]			Q1						
1595		[Q1]								
1597			Q1		[Q1]		Q1			
1598			●Q2			●Q1	●Q2 ●Q3		Q1	
1599					Q2				●Q2	
1600	[Q2]	[Q2]		Q2				●Q1		●Q1
1602			●Q3							
1603										
1604									●Q3	
1605			●Q4							
1608							●Q4		●Q4	
1609					Q3					
1611				Q3						
1612			●Q5							
1613									●Q5	
1615							●Q5			
1619	●[Q3] n.d.	●[Q3] n.d.						●Q2 1600		●Q2 1600

[bad texts enclosed in brackets]
●title-page ascription to Shakespeare

Much Ado	Henry IV Part 2	Merry Wives	Henry V	Hamlet	Troilus and Cressida	King Lear	Pericles	(Yorkshire Tragedy)	(London Prodigal)	(Oldcastle Part 1)	
											1594
											1595
											1597
											1598
											1599
●Q1	●Q1		[Q1]							Q1	1600
		●[Q1]	[Q2]								1602
				●[Q1]							1603
				● Q2							1604
									●Q1		1605
						●Q1		●Q1			1608
					●Q1	●Q1					1609
							●Q2				1609
					●Q3		●Q3				1611
											1612
											1613
											1615
			[Q3]			●Q2				●Q2	
	●[Q2]		1608			1608	●Q4	●Q2		1600	1619

the copy used for the First Folio had either been returned to the King's Men or disposed of otherwise. The successor to Cotes was Philip Chetwind, whose Third Folio (1663), as first issued, was again merely a reprint of its predecessor; but in a second issue the following year it was enlarged by two separately paginated additional sections amounting to one hundred twenty pages. The first contained *The much admired Play, called Pericles . . . Written by W. Shakespeare, and published in his life time.* Pericles had been frequently performed before the eighteen-year stage blackout, had gone through six quarto editions by 1635, and was the first Shakespeare play to be revived (by Thomas Betterton, with great success) when the theater was restored in 1660 along altered social lines. Chetwind's second additional section consisted of six other plays, all of them non-Shakespearean. Although mid-century booksellers' catalogs had already falsely ascribed no less than a dozen additional plays to Shakespeare, Chetwind showed some restraint by confining himself merely to plays that had appeared in print before 1616 (or so he thought, being in one case misled by a false Pavier date) and had carried a title-page ascription either to Shakespeare (*A Yorkshire Tragedy, The London Prodigal, Sir John Oldcastle*) or merely to a "W. S." (*Locrine*, 1595; *Thomas Lord Cromwell*, 1602; *The Puritan*, 1607).

All forty-three plays were then routinely included in the Fourth Folio (1685) by the booksellers who acquired Chetwind's property. The folio editions did not, however, eliminate the market for handier quarto editions of popular single plays, and about a dozen of the plays were separately republished between the First Folio of 1623 and the turn of the century. Stage popularity is reflected in the printing of five editions of *Othello* between 1655 and 1705 and six of *Hamlet* between 1676 and 1703. Certain of these late quartos, including *Macbeth* in 1673 and *Julius Caesar* in 1684, were reprinted from the folios (there being no other text), but certain others were reprinted instead from various pre-1623 quartos and preserved their different readings. The 1623 Folio text of *Hamlet,* for example, while adding about ninety lines that had not been published before, left out about 220 lines which appeared first in the Second Quarto of 1604 and which were successively preserved in all nine quarto reprints down to 1703. The longest dramatic episode embraced in that statistic is Hamlet's dialogue with the Norwegian captain and the ensuing "How all occasions . . . " soliloquy ("What is a man/ If his chief good and market of his time/ Be but to sleep and feed?"). Absent from all the folios, the episode was conspicuous enough to be brought to public attention in the first collected edition designed to replace them.

In the early 1700's Jacob Tonson secured the printing rights to Shakespeare's plays, planned a new six-volume octavo edition to replace the bulky 1685 Folio, and employed the dramatist Nicholas Rowe (paying him £ 36 10s) to prepare it. In addition to providing the first biography of Shakespeare, Rowe introduced a number of significant textual features, ranging from emendations of particular passages (Macbeth's "I dare do all that may become a man;/ Who dares do more is none," for example, results from Rowe's brilliant correction of "no more" in the folios) all the way to the general provision of location notes in scene headings, a convenience for a reading public that by Rowe's time had long been accustomed to pictorial staging within the frame of a proscenium arch. The textual priority to which Rowe himself drew attention in his prefatory pages, however, must have seemed more startling to some of his readers in 1709: "in some of the editions, especially the last [the 1685 Folio], there were many lines (and in *Hamlet* one whole scene) left out altogether; these are now all supplied." Rowe had in fact relied on the Fourth Folio as the main source of his edition, but he had consulted late-quarto texts for a few plays *(Hamlet, Othello, Romeo and Juliet)* and from them restored substantial passages that were not to be found in the folios. His dependence upon the Fourth Folio (even to retaining all the plays added by Chetwind) meant that his own text would inherit some progressive corruptions,[8] but by calling attention to variant texts of even a few plays (and restoring features as prominent as the Prologue to *Romeo and Juliet* to the collected edition) he was at least pointing in the required editorial direction. Apart from Rowe's text, Tonson provided forty-five engravings which illustrated episodes from the plays within the *mise-en-scène* of the current stage. This edition (published twice in 1709 and again in 1714) served the market until a few years after Rowe's death in 1718. Alexander Pope then arranged with Tonson to do the next collected Shakespeare, and he saw that he must start out, as Rowe so conspicuously had not, with identifying and acquiring

8. Thus, in the last act of *The Comedy of Errors,* Adriana, in the correct original text of 1623, speaks of her "important letters" from the Duke; in the later folios there occurs first the misprint "impoteant" and then the mis-correction "impotent," the 1685 reading whose defective sense prompted Rowe to emend to "all-potent." Shakespeare's word was restored by Pope in 1725.

as many of the earliest Shakespeare editions as he could locate.

"Though to explain and illustrate the writings of our poet is a principal duty of his editor, to ascertain his genuine text, to fix what is to be explained," wrote Edmond Malone in the Preface to his edition of 1790, "is his first and immediate object: and till it be established which of the ancient copies is entitled to preference, we have no criterion by which the text can be ascertained." Malone saw that this principle had not been sufficiently recognized in the editions of Pope (1725) or his immediate successors — Theobald (1733), Hanmer (1744), or Warburton (1747) — and that their texts were historically illiterate:

> When Mr. Pope first undertook the task of revising these plays, every anomaly of language, and every expression that was not understood at the time, were considered as errors or corruptions, and the text was altered, or amended, as it was called, at pleasure. The principal writers of the early part of this century seem never to have looked behind them, and to have considered their own era and their own phraseology as the standard of perfection: hence, from the time of Pope's edition, for above twenty years, to alter Shakespeare's text and to restore it, were considered as synonymous terms.

From Malone's vantage point, the next generation of editors — Johnson (1765), Capell (1768), Steevens (1773), and Malone himself — could be seen to operate within a much more fully articulated critical and historical framework. Its elements included Johnson's commentaries, the systematic comparison of early texts by Capell, the recovery and publication by Capell and Steevens of manuscript entries relevant to Shakespeare from the preserved records of the Stationers' Company, and Steevens' unusual republication of twenty early quarto texts, together with the first broad inquiries into Shakespeare's sources, the chronology of his plays, and the theatrical history of his times. During the pioneer generation "a true and correct edition" like Hanmer's could deliberately expunge from its text of *Henry V* an entire scene (the one scene Shakespeare wrote in French, Princess Katherine's English lesson in Act III) which the editor thought deplorable. The later generation had a more confident sense of textual responsibility:

> During the last thirty years our principal employment has been to *restore,* in the true sense of the word; to eject the arbitrary and capricious innovations made by our predecessors from ignorance of the phraseology and customs of the age in which Shakespeare lived.

Although the reorientation that occurred during the century is more complex than Malone's summary can express, it can be illustrated by comparing the conditions of the text in the versions of Pope and the editions of Malone's day.

By Malone's criteria Pope rather than Rowe was the first true editor, in the sense that he was the first editor who sought to determine his text by ignoring derivative reprints and seeking out the original editions (permitting him to clear away routine corruption of the kind seen in the textual descent, as shown in note 8, of Adriana's "important letters"). Eventually he acquired or made use of twenty-nine pre-1623 quartos, together with copies of both the First and Second Folios. (Johnson was the earliest editor to see clearly that variant readings in the Second Folio, however attractively they might sometimes fit their dramatic context, carried no authority beyond the printing-house.) On Pope's behalf Tonson in 1722 placed advertisements soliciting pre-1620 editions of several plays found only in the Folio. (Only when Capell quoted the 8 November 1623 Stationers' Register entry listing the manuscripts of plays about to be newly published in the Folio did it become obvious that no earlier editions of these plays were likely to turn up.) Pope had clearly been aware of the fatal defect in Rowe's performance and, with a more generous stipend from Tonson (£217 12s) and the editorial assistance — paid for by Tonson — of two friends (John Gay and Elijah Fenton), he set out conscientiously to repair it. He undertook the edition, once he had completed his six-year project of translating *The Iliad,* "merely because" (as he said in a later note to *The Dunciad*) he "thought nobody else would," and he spent "nearly two years" of the four he was at work on it "in the drudgery of comparing impressions." The edition that resulted, and the conclusions about Shakespeare's text that Pope promulgated in his Preface and notes, were inevitably of much greater consequence to his successors (either for emulation or rejection) than the slenderly prepared re-editing of the Fourth Folio produced by Rowe.

Among the quartos printed in Shakespeare's lifetime Pope found many passages (hundreds of lines in the 1608 *King Lear* in particular) that were manifestly authentic but had not been included in the folios or uncovered by Rowe, and these discoveries naturally tended to make him discount the authority of Hemmings and Condell. On the other hand, he also encountered a few quarto texts that were manifestly inferior to their Folio counterparts, like the garbled and abridged quarto versions of *Henry V* and *Henry VI Parts 2 and 3,* but these — in one of the great seminal blunders in the history of explaining Shakespeare's text — he conceived to be crude early versions of plays that Shakespeare had come later to enlarge and revise.[9] The bad quarto texts had in fact been singled out for exposure by Hemmings and Condell in their Folio preface "To the Great Variety of Readers":

> as where (before) you were abus'd with diverse stolne, and surreptitious copies, maimed, and deformed by the frauds and stealthes of injurious imposters, that expos'd them: even those, are now offer'd to your view cur'd, and perfect of their limbes . . .

But Pope interpreted "diverse" (several) to mean "all," ascribing to Hemmings and Condell an assertion they never made, "that all the other editions [before the Folio] were stolen and surreptitious," thus subverting their words and leaving Pope free to treat nearly all of the early quarto and Folio texts with undifferentiated disrespect. The "almost innumerable errors" that Pope saw generally throughout the early texts "have arisen from one source, the ignorance of the players, both as his actors, and as his editors." Thus, although he thought it had become "impossible to repair the injuries already done" ("too much time has elapsed, and the materials are too few"), Pope gave himself license to correct, improve, and refine the text of the plays at will.

9. In his Table of editions consulted, Pope cited the quartos of *Henry VI* as giving a "first sketch" of the Folio plays. Of *Henry V* he possessed the 1600 and "1608" (1619 Pavier) quartos, commenting that they "are short in many scenes and speeches, and want the Chorus's; which (with many other noble improvements) were since added by the Author, not above eight years before his death." Although he observed correctly in the headnote to his text that *Henry V* "was writ (as appears from a passage in the Chorus to the fifth Act) at the time of the Earl of Essex's commanding the forces in Ireland, in the reign of Q. Elizabeth" (i.e. 1599), he maintained at the same time (in the very next note) that "all the Chorus's were . . . added since the edition of 1608."

Pope confined his edition to the thirty-six plays of the First Folio, rejecting all seven of the plays added by Chetwind (including *Pericles*) as spurious. He recorded and even endorsed a "tradition" (which presumably reached him through Betterton) that *The Two Noble Kinsmen* was entirely by Shakespeare, but he left it out of his edition anyway. Theobald, Hanmer, Warburton, Johnson, and Capell acquiesced in these decisions, and the question of the proper canonical limits to the collected works (including the poems) was not effectively examined until Malone and Steevens addressed their talents to it at the end of the century. The thirty-six plays that Pope included, however, he revised with far more particular care, especially metrical care, than they had ever been given by anyone since Shakespeare.

Rowe's life of Shakespeare had been written to serve as the introduction to his edition, and its closing pages were given to identifying "some of those things I have been pleased with in looking him [Shakespeare] over." Possibly it was in response to such prompting that Pope invented the most visible idiosyncrasy of his edition: "Some of the most shining passages are distinguished by commas in the margin; and where the beauty lay not in particulars, but in the whole, a star is prefixed to the scene. This seems to me a shorter and less ostentatious method of performing the better half of criticism (namely, the pointing out an author's excellencies) than to fill a whole paper with citations of fine passages, with *general applauses* or *empty exclamations* at the tail of them." Equally visible and arresting, and a good deal less innocuous, was Pope's treatment of what he singled out as "suspected passages, which are excessively bad." Some 1500 lines of such "trash" (of which the most famous make up the episode with the Porter in *Macbeth,* filled with indecorous language) "are degraded to the bottom of the page." Both the "shining passages" and those "degraded" to the margin are of permanent interest mainly as an index to Pope's taste in Shakespeare; the rejected passages also provided unfortunate precedents for a few later critical judgments, such as Coleridge's that the Porter's "low" speeches had been "written for the mob by some other hand, perhaps with Shakespeare's consent." As a whole, however, they merely illustrate the judicial spirit in which Pope carried out his further line-by-line operations upon the text. With respect to its long-range implications for the shape of the received text, the most important single feature of Pope's edition — quite as extensive as the starred and degraded passages combined, although much less immediately visible to the reader — was his introduction of elaborate metrical reconstructions into the text of nearly all the plays.

Where Pope encountered two widely divergent texts, like the excellent Folio text of *Henry V* and the derivative quarto abridgment published in 1600, he did not try to determine "which of the ancient copies is entitled to preference"; he made free use of both as the basis of his own revision. After Bardolph's execution is reported to the King by Fluellen, Henry (in the correct Folio version) replies in prose:

> Wee would have all such offendors so cut off: and we give expresse charge, that in our Marches through the Countrey, there be nothing compell'd from the Villages; nothing taken, but pay'd for: none of the French upbrayded or abused in disdainefull Language; for when Le[n]itie and Crueltie play for a Kingdome, the gentler Gamester is the soonest winner.

The quarto version, regarded by Pope as an authentic "first draft" by Shakespeare and by modern critics as resulting from the distortions of an aural report,[10] had been cut and altered verbally as well as turned into a rough sort of verse:
> We would have all offendors so cut off,
> And we here give expresse commaundment,
> That there be nothing taken from the villages but paid for,
> None of the French abused,
> Or abraided with disdainfull language:
> For when cruelty and lenitie play for a Kingdome,
> The gentlest gamester is the sooner winner.

Pope draws even-handedly from both versions (except

---

10. A present-day instance of such accidental distortion appears in the transcript of the United States Senate "Watergate" Hearings of October 4, 1973. A young witness who had been involved in slandering political candidates was asked by Senator Ervin if he had ever encountered this passage from Shakespeare:
> Good name in man and woman, dear my lord,
> Is the immediate jewel of their souls.
> Who steals my purse steals trash: 'tis something, nothing;
> 'Twas mine, 'tis his, and has been slave to thousands:
> But he that filches from me my good name
> Robs me of that which not enriches him,
> And makes me poor indeed.

The Senator's letter-perfect reading of Iago's speech to Othello is preserved on videotape, but through the stenographic medium the official published transcript (p. 4397) is marked by the mis-hearings, omissions, and metrical stigmata found typically in reported texts:
> Good name in man and woman, dear lord, is the immediate juror
>   of their souls;
> Who steals my purse steals trash;
> Tis something, nothing.
> Twas mine,
> Tis his, and has been a slave to thousands.
> But he that filches from me my good name,
> Robs me of that which not enriches him and makes poor indeed.

where the quarto reading is clearly inferior in sense) to produce his own careful pentameter verse paragraph:

> We would have such offenders so cut off,
> And give express charge that in all our march
> There shall be nothing taken from the villages
> But shall be paid for, and no *French* upbraided
> Or yet abused in disdainful language;
> When lenity and cruelty play for kingdoms,
> The gentler gamester is the soonest winner.

This artful rearrangement probably bears some relation to the declamatory acting styles of Pope's generation. If as an "edition" of Shakespeare it amounts to outright revision, Pope was fortified by the premises he held about Hemmings and Condell ("prose from verse they did not know"), and he saw himself in the role of literary executor (as David Nichol Smith has pointed out), merely polishing up Shakespeare's otherwise disordered remains into decorous, if not quite Augustan, form.[11]

In the case of plays that had not been published before the First Folio, where Pope did not have to face and choose between variant arrangements of verse and prose, he was, nevertheless, just as attentive to the task of perfecting Shakespeare's meter as he had been in handling the disparate versions of *Henry V*. Perhaps the most remarkable example is his treatment of *Macbeth*. Despite his rejection of the Porter episode and a few shorter passages, Pope appears, from the number of stars and commas he affixed to the text, to have held it in higher esteem than any other play. The best of his emendations (as when Macbeth describes Murder moving "with Tarquin's ravishing strides," where "sides" had been the reading of the folios and Rowe) are beyond cavil;

---

11. *Shakespeare in the Eighteenth Century* (1928), p. 34.

nevertheless, he made the mistake of deferring to a few variant readings from the Second Folio, such as one that actually alters Macbeth's "all our yesterdays have lighted fools / The way to dusty death" to read " . . . the way to study death" ("a reading which," as John Butt says, "emphasizes morality at the expense of poetry").[12] But his most elaborate effort went into splitting up and reconstructing the verse-lines, on a scale that far surpassed the occasional tinkering with meter in the later folios and Rowe. One example is the following passage — the opening of Act I, Scene 4 (where the audience is waiting for Macbeth's succession to the title of Cawdor):

(First Folio)
  Flourish. Enter King, Lenox, Malcolme, Donalbaine, and Attendants.
   King. Is execution done on *Cawdor?*
Or not those in Commission yet return'd?
   Mal. My Liege, they are not yet come back.
But I have spoke with one that saw him die:
Who did report, that very frankly hee
Confess'd his Treasons, implor'd your Highnesse Pardon,
And set forth a deep Repentance:
Nothing in his Life became him,
Like the leaving it. Hee dy'de,
As one that had been studied in his death,
To throw away the dearest thing he ow'd
As 'twere a carelesse Trifle.

(Pope Edition)
   King. Is execution done on *Cawdor* yet?
Are not those in commission yet return'd?
   Mal. My liege,
They are not yet come back. But I have spoke
With one that saw him die, who did report
That very frankly he confess'd his treasons,

12. *Pope's Taste in Shakespeare* (1936), p. 8.

> Implor'd your highness' pardon, and set forth
> A deep repentance; nothing in his life
> Became him like the leaving it. He dy'd,
> As one that had been studied in his death, . . .

The "yet" in the first line is an addition by Pope, no doubt to fill up the meter rather than modify the sense. The change of "Or" to "Are" in the second line originated with the Second Folio. The rearrangements in the next six lines — similar ones appear in 76 other speeches elsewhere (out of about 360 verse speeches of one or more lines in the entire play) — show his confident skill in creating a new metrical order, although his occasional conversions of prose passages into pentameter verse throughout the canon probably required even greater poetic self-confidence.

Textual criticism has been narrowly defined as the removal of error from an author's text, and Pope's Shakespeare became the first English martyr to the cause. The tone of Lewis Theobald's 1726 treatise *Shakespeare Restored* was not as abrasive as its subtitle, *a Specimen of the many errors, as well committed, as unamended, by Mr. Pope in his late edition of this poet,* but this "first essay of literal criticism upon any author in the English tongue" (as Theobald called it), by following the precedents of classical scholars like Richard Bentley, raised standards for textual emendation to a degree that made Pope's amateur status and several key defects of his edition immediately apparent — and embarrassing enough to Pope for him to memorialize "piddling Theobald" in verse. The most famous of all Shakespearean emendations, Theobald's correction of the anomalous phrase (in the folios and Rowe) with which the Hostess in Act II of *Henry*

V describes the dying Falstaff, "his Nose was as sharpe as a pen, and a Table of greene fields" — which in *Shakespeare Restored* became " . . . and a' babbled of green fields" — was set off against Pope's decision to delete the phrase on the supposition that a property note, calling for a table kept by a hypothetical stagehand named Greenfield, had gotten itself into the dialogue. Both by its examples and the classic precepts it brought to the text — such as the use of parallel passages to clear up difficulties ("every author is best expounded and explained in *one* place, by his own usage and manner of expression in *others*") — *Shakespeare Restored* pointed the way to a superior text. With the exclusive Tonson copyright in Shakespeare due to expire in 1731 (according to the copyright statute in effect since 1710) and with competing booksellers courting him, Theobald secured a generous contract with the Tonson firm in 1730 (£ 652 10s plus other emoluments), and his edition appeared three years later.

The exiled passages were recalled from the margins, most of the word-changes introduced by Pope to trim or pad lines (like "yet" in Duncan's speech) were removed, widespread readings from the early editions that Pope had either not seen or possibly misunderstood (like Duncan's "Or") were restored, and explanations of Shakespearean usage were supported, for the first time, by reference to literature of his age. The Theobald edition, however, had been set in type from a marked copy of the Pope edition, and whatever changes Pope had effected that Theobald positively approved — or did not venture to challenge, or did not notice — were silently adopted. Theobald's Preface and many of his notes continued to score points against

Pope, so that wherever his text was in actual agreement with Pope's alterations — the intricate revision of *Henry V*, the re-linings of verse (as in Malcolm's speech), the conversion of prose to verse — these alterations bore the apparent endorsement of Pope's sharpest editorial adversary and were generally preserved (apart from small disagreements on how best to versify some passages of prose)[13] in the editions of Hanmer, Warburton, and Johnson.

With the 1768 edition by Edward Capell, however, came a number of new editorial departures. Capell, by his own account, had been spurred to edit Shakespeare by "indignation" at the slapdash methods of Hanmer. He began in the 1740's to collect materials, eventually locating over twice as many of the quartos as were known to Pope, with a view to reconstructing the text of the plays on a new foundation. In his Introduction he distinguished between those quartos that he thought had been printed from "either the poet's first draughts, or else imperfect and stolen copies" (in either case lacking authority) and those quartos that were printed from authoritative manuscripts and were therefore preferable (owing to cumulative errors in reprinting) to their descendant Folio texts. Thus he was able to discard as a source the bad text of *Henry V* and edit the play from the Folio version

13. Thus Pope had taken two sentences from a speech to Hotspur by his wife in Act II of *Henry IV Part 1* — "Out you mad-headed ape, a weasel hath not such a deal of spleen as you are tossed with. In faith I'll know your business Harry, that I will." — and, deleting "Harry," printed them as three verse-lines ending . . . not . . . with . . . will; "Harry" was restored by Hanmer with verses ending . . . hath . . . with . . . will; Johnson deleted "Harry" again and redivided into four lines ending . . . ape . . . spleen . . . with . . . will.

for the first time since Rowe. He was also able to place a new reliance on the good quartos where his analysis showed the Folio texts to be derived from them. One such text is the 1597 First Quarto of *Richard II;* the handling of one brief passage from it, described below, provides a fair index to the nature of the changes in the received text effected by Capell.

The context is the dialogue between the senior gardener and his man (Act III, Scene 4) about "our sea-walled garden, the whole land," and the fate of King Richard:

He that h[at]h suffered this disordered spring,
Hath now himselfe met with the fall of leafe:
The weedes which his broad spreading leaves did shelter,
That seemde in eating him to hold him up,
Are pluckt up roote and all by Bullingbrooke,
I meane the Earle of Wiltshire, Bushie, Greene.
   Man. What are they dead?
   Gard. They are.
And Bullingbrooke hath ceasde the wastefull king;
Oh what pitie is it that he had not so trimde,   *a*
And drest his land as we this garden at time of yeare   *b*
Do wound the barke, the skinne of our fruit trees,   *c*
Lest being over prowd in sap and bloud,
With too much riches it confound it selfe . . .

The text of lines *a* to *c* is sound enough here, but (with punctuation after "it," "land," and "garden" having been added by the Third Quarto) the Folio reprinted them as follows:

Oh, what pitty is it, that he had not so trim'd
And drest his Land, as we this Garden, at time of yeare,
And wound the Barke, . . .

With "and" replacing the verb in line *c*, this nonsense survived through all the folios and into Rowe. Pope was the first to stick at it. He seems also to have stuck at the phrase "at time of year" (which means "in season"),

since he deported it to the margin, and at the overflowing measure of the lines, for he pruned them down to regulation length:
> What pity is it, that he had not trimm'd
> And drest his land; as we this garden dress,
> And wound the bark, . . .

This revision (or Theobald's slight variant of it, putting back "so" in line a and contracting "is it" to "is't") was reprinted down through the Johnson edition, but Capell, characteristically, restored most of the original wording while rearranging the lines (following editorial custom since Pope) into a kind of platonic pentameter:
> 1.*S.* What, are they dead?
> *Gar.* They are; and *Bolingbroke*
> Hath seiz'd the wasteful king. What pity is it,
> That he had not so trim'd and dress'd his land,
> As we this garden! We, at time of year,
> Do wound the bark, . . .

The division into two sentences and the redundant "We" are essential to Capell's meter, and in this form (with Malone later restoring the "Oh" before "what pity") his arrangement passed into the received text. The Capell edition generally made a sharp break with its predecessors in going back to the newly sorted-out original texts, but not with their established precedent of fine-tuning the versification. If anything Capell was even more meticulous than Pope in this respect. Thus in the *Macbeth* passage cited earlier he converted the opening lines into two tidy verses — "*King.* Is execution done on Cawdor? Are not/ Those in commission yet return'd? *Malc.* My liege," — while keeping Pope's arrangement in the rest.

Theobald, Hanmer, and Warburton had started the custom of providing various forms of editorial commentary in footnotes running through the text, and the range of annotation was extended in the Johnson edition of 1765 to include critical summations at the end of each play. Johnson's Preface (called by Adam Smith "the most manly piece of criticism that was ever published") and his superior commentaries led to the immediate reprinting of his edition. When the Capell edition (under way long before Johnson's appeared) came out in 1768, in the form of ten volumes of text without any notes (which Capell announced he would publish separately afterwards) it failed to reach a second printing. Its textual superiority, nevertheless, was perfectly evident to Johnson's designated successor, George Steevens. In preparing his revised text of the plays for the Johnson-Steevens edition of 1773, even before the first volume of Capell's notes had come out, Steevens appropriated most of Capell's reformations. In the Gardener's speech, for example, where the 1765 Johnson text had followed Pope, the 1773 Johnson-Steevens followed Capell's rearrangement with great precision (changing only one line, "As we this garden! We, at time of year," to read "As we this garden, who at times of year"). The general shape of the thirty-six plays remained, similarly, in much the form they had taken with Capell, through the later "Johnson Shakespeares" (the Johnson-Steevens editions of 1773 and 1778 and the Johnson-Steevens-Reed edition of 1785) and into the Malone edition of 1790. The most substantial change in the received text during this era was its enlargement to include the poems and *Pericles* after they had been edited and their cases argued by Malone and Steevens in Malone's 1780 *Supplement* to the Johnson-Steevens edition of 1778. The possibility of adding *The Two Noble Kinsmen* was considered in the same volume by Steevens, but after observing that "the language and images of this piece coincide perpetually with those in the dramas of Shakespeare," he came to the conclusion that it had been written entirely by Fletcher in silent imitation of Shakespeare. His argument (and Malone's silent concurrence) effectively excluded it from collected editions of Shakespeare until well into the nineteenth century.

It was Steevens also who introduced a new kind of typographic verse-measurement into the printing of Shakespeare's plays. He rearranged the text of all thirty-seven plays in his 1793 edition so that the short lines of succeeding speeches would, wherever feasible, appear as component parts of ten-syllable verse-lines — as in the courteous exchange that follows from Act II, Scene 2 of *Antony and Cleopatra,* after Lepidus has asked Caesar and Antony to let "what's amiss" between them be "gently heard" and Antony has warmly agreed. (The first arrangement below, from the 1623 Folio, was preserved through all editions down to 1790; the Steevens arrangement beneath it disposes the eleven syllables of the five speeches into one presumed verse-line and a one-syllable nondescript.)

(1)
Caes. Welcome to Rome.
Ant. Thanke you.
Caes. Sit.
Ant. Sit sir.
Caes. Nay then.

(2)
Caes. Welcome to Rome.
Ant.   Thank you.
Caes.   Sit.
Ant.   Sit, sir!
Caes.   Nay,
    Then —

The 1793 Steevens edition generally preserved the basic metrical form of the eighteenth-century text as it was first shaped by Pope and then reshaped mainly by Capell, but extended its range, making use of what may be called metrical white space, to encompass several thousand shorter lines that previous editors had been content to print without any indentations. This new metrical typography of Steevens was retained, after Steevens died in 1800, in the 21-volume Johnson-Steevens-Reed editions of 1803 and 1813 and, with modifications, in the more important 21-volume Malone-Boswell edition of 1821 (called by Sir Edmund Chambers "the final word of eighteenth-century scholarship on Shakespeare"). In carrying out the work of Malone after his death in 1812, the 1821 editor, James Boswell the younger, contributed an essay on verse tradition since Chaucer in which he criticized Steevens for his failure to appreciate, in Shakespeare and other Elizabethan dramatists, the common use of half-lines, alexandrines, and other departures from the ten-syllable "modern standard" to which Steevens was addicted. Apart, however, from re-positioning some of the metrical white space and restoring a number of words that Steevens had sacrificed to an idealized meter, the text in the Malone-Boswell edition generally embraced the Steevens typography and dressed out the plays in much the final form to which a standard line-numbering was at last applied in the Cambridge Shakespeare of the 1860's.

In the common instance of a part-line conclusion to one speech combining with the part-line beginning of the next to form a single pentameter, the white-space indentation may appear harmless and textually inconsequential. But the actual effect of Steevens' innovation in conjunction with the earlier metrical history of the text may be observed in the parallel versions, reproduced in the following photographic insert, of *Antony and Cleopatra*, Act III, Scene 3, the Alexandrian scene in which the Messenger who saw Octavia in Rome returns for his second interview with Cleopatra (after having barely escaped with his life from the first). The Folio mixture of verse and prose provides our only authoritative source for the rhythms in which the speeches may be realized. The words of the dialogue in the standardized editorial version have been changed only in spelling, but of the forty-seven editorial lines of presumed verse that make up the scene as a whole, the collational notes in the Cambridge Shakespeare attribute the metrical construction of no fewer than twenty-four lines to as many as six different editorial sources — two lines (31-32) to the Third Folio, five to Rowe (18-19, 44-46), seven to Pope (2-5, 41-43), five to Theobald (6-7, 22-24), three to Capell (8-10), and two to Steevens (26-27). (Steevens was also responsible for the arrangement of lines 1, 11, 21, 25, 33, 37, and 40 as single verses.) Despite the self-evident precision in this patient metrical grooming, as many as ten of the resulting forty-seven lines — three taken over intact from the Folio (28, 30, 47) and seven worked up by editors (2, 8, 26, 31, 32, 43, 44) — still cannot be scanned as iambic pentameter, the presumed rationale and chief goal in this century-long cultivation of the lines.

 The essential sources that lay open to the founders of the Cambridge Shakespeare, William George Clark and John Glover, included the library of early editions collected by Capell, which he had bequeathed intact to Trinity College. Unlike Capell they drew on this material not so much to reconstruct the received text as to make accessible, through the concisely footnoted grid of variant readings from all pre-1700 and selected post-1700 editions, its authoritative documentation. "The novelty of its plan," they say in their 1863 Preface, "will exempt us from all suspicion of a design to supersede, or even compete with, the many able and learned Editors who have preceded us in the same field." Since one of their public-service goals was "to number the lines in each scene separately, so as to facilitate reference," the line-numbered text of the nine-volume Cambridge edition (1863-66) was made available at the same time, without the footnoted textual apparatus, in the one-volume Globe edition (1864), providing the act, scene, and line numbering that has been standard in most modern-spelling editions and reference literature ever since. (Accidental misnumberings were corrected in the 1891-93 revision by William Aldis Wright, who had replaced Glover as Clark's co-editor after Volume I in the original edition.)

The textual fate of one reading at the closing moment of *Henry IV Part 1* suggests the beneficial kind of change brought about by the Cambridge Shakespeare. Just before the lines of the King that end the play there is a two-line speech by Prince John of Lancaster, accepting from Hal the honor of delivering to Douglas his grant of freedom ("I thank your grace for this high courtesy / Which I shall give away immediately"). The speech appeared in the quartos — each serving as the printer's copy for the next — of 1598, 1599, 1604, and 1608, but it was left out of the quarto of 1613 and was not restored when a copy of the 1613 quarto was prepared for use by the Folio printer. As a consequence it did not make its reappearance in the

Antony and Cleopatra, Act III, Scene 3
(Folio and Cambridge texts):

 Enter Cleopatra, Charmian, Iras, and Alexas.
 Cleo. Where is the Fellow?
 Alex. Halfe afeard to come.
 Cleo. Go too, go too: Come hither Sir.
   Enter the Messenger as before.
 Alex. Good Maiestie: *Herod* of Iury dare not looke vpon you, but when you are well pleas'd.
 Cleo. That *Herods* head, Ile haue: but how? When *Anthony* is gone, through whom I might commaund it; Come thou neere.
 Mes. Most gratious Maiestie.
 Cleo. Did'st thou behold *Octauia*?
 Mes. I dread Queene.
 Cleo. Where?
 Mes. Madam in Rome, I lookt her in the face: and saw her led betweene her Brother, and *Marke Anthony*.
 Cleo. Is she as tall as me?
 Mes. She is not Madam.
 Cleo. Didst heare her speake?
Is she shrill tongu'd or low?
 Mes. Madam, I heard her speake, she is low voic'd.
 Cleo. That's not so good: he cannot like her long.
 Char. Like her? Oh *Isis*: 'tis impossible.
 Cleo. I thinke so *Charmian*: dull of tongue, & dwarfish What Maiestie is in her gate, remember If ere thou look'st on Maiestie.
 Mes. She creepes: her motion, & her station are as one: She shewes a body, rather then a life, A Statue, then a Breather.
 Cleo. Is this certaine?
 Mes. Or I haue no obseruance.
 Cha. Three in Egypt cannot make better note.
 Cleo. He's very knowing, I do perceiu't, There's nothing in her yet.

Enter CLEOPATRA, CHARMIAN, IRAS, *and* ALEXAS.

Cleo. Where is the fellow?
Alex. Half afeard to come.
Cleo. Go to, go to.

Enter Messenger.

Come hither, sir.
Alex. Good majesty,
Herod of Jewry dare not look upon you
But when you are well pleased.
Cleo. That Herod's head
I'll have: but how, when Antony is gone 5
Through whom I might command it? Come thou near.
Mess. Most gracious majesty,—
Cleo. Didst thou behold
Octavia?
Mess. Ay, dread queen.
Cleo. Where?
Mess. Madam, in Rome
I look'd her in the face, and saw her led
Between her brother and Mark Antony. 10
Cleo. Is she as tall as me?
Mess. She is not, madam.
Cleo. Didst hear her speak? is she shrill-tongued or low?
Mess. Madam, I heard her speak; she is low-voiced.
Cleo. That's not so good. He cannot like her long.
Char. Like her! O Isis! 'tis impossible. 15
Cleo. I think so, Charmian: dull of tongue and dwarfish.
What majesty is in her gait? Remember,
If e'er thou look'dst on majesty.
Mess. She creeps:
Her motion and her station are as one;
She shows a body rather than a life, 20
A statue than a breather.
Cleo. Is this certain?
Mess. Or I have no observance.
Char. Three in Egypt
Cannot make better note.
Cleo. He's very knowing;
I do perceive 't: there's nothing in her yet:

33

The Fellow ha's good iudgement.
Char. Excellent.
Cleo. Guesse at her yeares, I prythee.
Mess. Madam, she was a widdow.
Cleo. Widdow? *Charmian*, hearke.
Mes. And I do thinke she's thirtie.
Cle. Bear'st thou her face in mind? is't long or round?
Mess. Round, euen to faultinesse.
Cleo. For the most part too, they are foolish that are
so. Her haire what colour?
Mess. Browne Madam: and her forehead
As low as she would wish it.
Cleo. There's Gold for thee,
Thou must not take my former sharpenesse ill,
I will employ thee backe againe: I finde thee
Most fit for businesse. Go, make thee ready,
Our Letters are prepar'd.
Char. A proper man.
Cleo. Indeed he is so: I repent me much
That so I harried him. Why me think's by him,
This Creature's no such thing.
Char. Nothing Madam.
Cleo. The man hath seene some Maiesty, and should
know.
Char. Hath he seene Maiestie? *Isis* else defend: and
seruing you so long.
Cleopa. I haue one thing more to aske him yet good
Charmian: but 'tis no matter, thou shalt bring him to me
where I will write; all may be well enough.
Char. I warrant you Madam.   *Exeunt.*

The fellow has good judgement.
 Char.   Excellent.   25
 Cleo. Guess at her years, I prithee.
 Mess.   Madam.
She was a widow—
 Cleo.   Widow! Charmian, hark.
 Mess. And I do think she's thirty.
 Cleo. Bear'st thou her face in mind? is't long or round?
 Mess. Round even to faultiness.   30
 Cleo. For the most part, too, they are foolish that
    are so.
Her hair, what colour?
 Mess.   Brown, madam: and her forehead
As low as she would wish it.
 Cleo.   There's gold for thee.
Thou must not take my former sharpness ill:
I will employ thee back again; I find thee   35
Most fit for business: go make thee ready;
Our letters are prepared.   [*Exit Messenger.*
 Char.   A proper man.
 Cleo. Indeed, he is so: I repent me much
That so I harried him. Why, methinks, by him,
This creature's no such thing.
 Char.   Nothing, madam.   40
 Cleo. The man hath seen some majesty, and should
    know.
 Char. Hath he seen majesty? Isis else defend,
And serving you so long!
 Cleo. I have one thing more to ask him yet, good
    Charmian:
But 'tis no matter; thou shalt bring him to me   45
Where I will write. All may be well enough.
 Char. I warrant you, madam.   [*Exeunt.*

text before the eighteenth century, when Johnson (in Steevens' words) "judiciously suppose[d] it to have been rejected by Shakespeare himself," and even Capell, who had failed to ferret out the 1613 omission, half-apologized (in his 1774 notes) for restoring it: "The reply of prince John to his brother is inserted with some unwillingness: the folio's have it not, and possibly by the author's direction: thinking that what the prince has to say, might be better express'd in a bow, than by such a jingling and weak couplet as is given him here." For some fifty years thereafter the speech was usually printed apart from the text in reduced type — in the 1821 Malone-Boswell edition, for example, as part of a two-tiered footnote debating its merits (even though Boswell concluded that he "can see no reason for its rejection"). The Cambridge collation finally showed the 1613 quarto to have been a blind reprint of its predecessor, so that its two-line omission might be seen as merely the most prominent among a scattering of type-composing accidents; the speech was therefore restored to the text, the authority noted, and an authentic reading that involves an odd turn in the closing onstage ceremony was engraved in the received text with as much security of tenure as it had probably not enjoyed since before 1613.

One legacy of eighteenth-century learning was the effective discrimination between two classes of early quartos, signalized in the Cambridge Shakespeare by the publication of two versions for each of six plays. The modern-spelling editions of *Hamlet, Romeo and Juliet, Merry Wives of Windsor, Henry V,* and *Henry VI Parts 2 and 3* were based (as were the other thirty-one plays) on good quarto and Folio sources, but for each of them the Cambridge editors provided separately an exact reprint of the "imperfect" first quarto, with the collation of the descendant reprints (of *Merry Wives of Windsor* and the history plays, as shown in the table on pages 8-9) recorded underneath. All six quartos had been held at one time or another (since Pope) to be an "early sketch" of a play that Shakespeare later revised, but except for *Merry Wives of Windsor* the Cambridge editors no longer found such a view tenable. The manuscripts for *Hamlet, Romeo and Juliet, and Henry V* they surmised to be the work of reporters taking short-hand notes during performances, and they also spelled out (in their note on *Hamlet*) a scenario in which "some inferior actor or servant" might have been able to supplement his notes "by a reference to the authentic copy in the library of the theatre," although he "would necessarily work in haste and by stealth, and in any case would not be likely to work very conscientiously for the printer or bookseller who was paying him to deceive his masters."

For their explanation of the *Henry VI* quartos, however, the Cambridge editors had to accommodate a more complicated hypothesis. Neither the assumption of a "first sketch" (held by Pope) nor of a short-hand report (by which Johnson sought to account for these "mutilated" editions) had been easy to accept after Malone in 1787 brought out his *Dissertation* on the *Henry VI* plays. "Several passages and circumstances found in the old plays, of which there is no trace" in the Folio versions, persuaded Malone that such readings "could not have arisen from unskillful copyists or short-hand writers, who sometimes curtail and mutilate, but do not invent or amplify." In Malone's solution the quartos preserved inferior plays by other dramatists that Shakespeare at the beginning of his career revised and expanded into the plays printed in the Folio. The Cambridge editors said they could "neither agree with Malone on the one hand that they contain nothing of Shakespeare's, nor with Mr [Charles] Knight on the other hand that they are entirely his work"; but they did not question the essential position of Malone that *The First Part of the Contention* (1594) and *The True Tragedy of Richard Duke of York* (1595) were written before the Folio plays, maintaining that *Henry VI Part 2* had been "founded" on the former and that the latter had "formed the ground-work" of *Part 3*. Of the six "imperfect" quarto editions, three were thus referred to a period before Shakespeare revised them and three others to manuscripts put together by reporters (incited by corrupt booksellers) after the plays had been completed and performed.

When Pope came back from the first long exploration into the wilderness of early editions, he brought back with him, among other things, a blanket contempt for Hemmings and Condell, to whom he mistakenly attributed, in turn, a blanket condemnation of all editions previous to the Folio as stolen and surreptitious. The earliest editor able to single out the "spurious" quartos as a general class ("whose places were then supplied by true and genuine copies") had been Capell, and in unfair retrospect one might assume that this perception, along with his corollary identification of those good quartos that had served as Folio copy, should have led him to correct that worst of all Pope's mistakes. Instead he went along a path of less resistance and reconciled his observations with the older view, treating the fact that several good-quarto texts were used in printing the Folio — "the editions of plays preceding the folio, are the very basis of those we have there" — as shocking proof of the duplicity practiced by Hemmings and Condell in claiming (as they never had) to replace a market saturated with nothing but corrupt editions.

The same misrepresentation was reinforced by Malone in his 1790 Preface, where, after listing thirteen good and two bad quarto texts, he went on to assert that "the players, when they mention these copies, represent them all as mutilated and imperfect; but this was merely thrown out to give an additional value to their own edition, and is not strictly true of any but two of their number." In the 1863 Preface by Clark and Glover it had become an article of faith — "the natural inference to be drawn" from the statement by Hemmings and Condell "is, that all the separate editions of Shakespeare's plays were 'stolen,' 'surreptitious,' and 'imperfect' " — from which they drew the appropriate conclusion: "As the 'setters forth' are thus convicted of a 'suggestio falsi' in one point, it is not improbable that they may have been guilty of the like in another." Even after the early editions had been carefully sifted and the bad ones properly segregated, the Cambridge editors thus continued the depreciation of Hemmings and Condell that began with Pope. On the kind of manuscripts that might lie behind the printing of good texts they were silent more often than not, offering suggestions only when, as in the case of the six bad quartos, glaring anomalies of printing elicited their attention so as to demand some effort at explanation.

A prominent case in point is their consideration of *Timon of Athens,* which ends on page 98 in the Tragedies section of the Folio, followed by two unnumbered pages (one listing the personae of *Timon* and the second blank), then by the beginning of *Julius Caesar* on a page numbered 109:

> From this it may be inferred that for some reason the printing of *Julius Caesar* was commenced before that of *Timon* was finished. It may be that the manuscript of *Timon* was imperfect, and that the printing was stayed till it could be completed by some playwright engaged for the purpose. This would account for the manifest imperfections at the close of the play. But it is difficult to conceive how the printer came to miscalculate so widely the space required to be left.
>
> The well-known carelessness of the printers of the Folio in respect of metre will not suffice to account for the deficiencies of *Timon*. The original play, on which Shakespeare worked, must have been written, for the most part, either in prose or in very irregular verse.

Modern studies of the Folio printing have come to a very different conclusion about the page-numbering anomaly. *Troilus and Cressida* was first intended for the position between *Romeo and Juliet* and *Julius Caesar;* work was interrupted after a sheet containing the last page of *Romeo* and three pages of *Troilus* had been printed; plans for including *Troilus* in the Folio were abandoned (although later resumed after copyright difficulties were overcome); and the shorter manuscript of *Timon* was provided in its place. The metrical irregularities noted by the Cambridge editors are more pervasive in *Timon* than in any of the other Folio plays and are among the features that, for the past fifty years, many critics have taken as evidence that an unfinished draft of the play served as the printer's copy. In any event the suggestion by the Cambridge editors that "the printing was stayed till it could be completed by some playwright engaged for the purpose" indicates their easy use of Hemmings and Condell as a stalking horse, even while they had to concede that their suggestion was finally inadequate to account for "how the printer came to miscalculate so widely."

Of the six "imperfect" quartos printed by the Cambridge editors, the one that drew the most public attention, after a copy was first brought to light by Sir Henry Bunbury in 1823, was the First Quarto of *Hamlet* (1603). Messrs. Payne and Foss (booksellers) called their exact reprint of the 1603 text (1825) "this tragedy as originally written by Shakespeare." The initial objection to this view was that, even after allowing for accidental and inexplicable confusion, much of the writing was too impoverished to be Shakespeare's. By 1858, when the 1603 *Hamlet* quarto became the first printed book to be republished in a photo-lithographic facsimile, the early-sketch assumption had been replaced by the hypothesis, held by J. Payne Collier and later the Cambridge editors, that the poor text originated in a short-hand report financed by an unscrupulous bookseller. In 1880 the 1603 *Hamlet* became the first in a new series of forty-three Shakespeare quarto facsimiles, superintended by Frederick J. Furnivall (founder of the New Shakspere Society), with the Cambridge-Globe line-numbering (wherever precise correspondences between good and bad texts could be noted) printed in the margin. Among the close observations invited by this critical device was the fact (noted briefly by Furnivall in the course of a diffuse introduction) that the speeches of a few of the characters were consistently reported with greater fidelity to the good text than the speeches of others.

The theory that the Bad Quartos (as Alfred Pollard named them in 1909) originated in actors' memorial reporting — an action that had no necessary connection with any booksellers until the manuscript had outlived its theatrical use — was developed along several complementary lines of theatrical and textual research in the first three decades of this century. When Malone found passages in the Bad Quarto of *Henry VI Part 2* for which no counterparts could be found in the Folio text, he asked (in a note to Act I, Scene 3), "what spurious copy, or imperfect transcript taken in short-hand, ever produced such variations as these?" The answer, although it lay dormant until the twentieth century, was produced by Steevens: "Such varieties, during several years, were to be found in every MS. copy of Mr. Sheridan's then unprinted Duenna, as used in country theatres. The dialogue of it was obtained piece-meal, and connected by frequent interpolations." One of the counterfeit versions of *The Duenna,* performed at Birmingham in 1776, was prepared by Tate Wilkinson,[14] whose motive he disclosed in the *Memoirs of His Own Life* (1790): "The fashion of not publishing is quite modern, and the favorite pieces not being printed, but kept under lock and key, is of infinite prejudice to us poor devils in the country theatres, as we really cannot afford to pay for the purchase of MSS." Another actor, John Bernard, who played Sir Benjamin Backbite in performances of *The School for Scandal* at

14. The history of the Sheridan theatrical piracies (and the intricate bibliography of the variant texts that were published) was illuminated by R. Crompton Rhodes in his 1928 edition of Sheridan, and the history of the *Henry VI* texts by Peter Alexander in *Shakespeare's "Henry VI" and "Richard III"* (1929). The extracts below from Wilkinson (*Memoirs, II,* 230) and John Bernard (*Retrospections of the Stage* [1830], I, 207-209), first reprinted by Rhodes, may also be found in the Cecil Price edition of Sheridan (1973).

Bath in 1778, described the climate for exploiting the legally unprotected stage rights of any magnetic play: "Its success at Bath had dispersed its fame about the West of England, and it was highly probable that, if the play were produced at Exeter, it would run a number of nights to full houses. But the comedy was not yet published, and the managers, who had copies of it, had obtained them on condition that they did not permit the same to become the parent of others. This was a precaution of Sheridan's, not with any view of emolument, but in order to preserve his language from mutilation, and prevent the play from being produced at any theatre where the proper attention could not be paid to its 'getting up.' " Bernard also described how, with the aid of his wife (who had played both Lady Teazle and Mrs. Candour) and the loan of two manuscript parts from actor-friends (who had played Joseph and Sir Oliver), he made "a compilation of the comedy" and supplied the manuscript of his reconstruction to the manager of the Exeter and West of England Company.

Another theatrical document, chronologically closer to the Bad Quartos, is the portion that survives of Edward Alleyn's part (apparently based on the prompt-copy and corrected in Alleyn's hand) as Orlando, preserving about two-thirds of his speeches and cues, in Robert Greene's *Orlando Furioso*. The play was probably first acted in the autumn of 1591, and a badly abridged text was published in 1594. The actor's part was left by Alleyn among other documents (including the account-books of his father-in-law Philip Henslowe's theatrical management) in the custody of the institution he founded, the College of God's Gift at Dulwich, in 1619. It was first compared closely with such corresponding lines as survive in the mutilated 1594 text by Sir Walter Greg, whose *Two Elizabethan Stage Abridgements* (Malone Society, 1923) reproduced both the text and the part and annotated the heavy cutting, verbal corruption, traces of oral transmission, and occasional interpolations by the abridger-adapter in the 1594 perversion of Orlando's role. The key element in the Pollard-Greg-Rhodes-Alexander case was memory, and it explained such previously difficult data as the sudden appearance, in the middle of what would otherwise look like only a badly rendered report of a Shakespeare speech, of some additional matter apparently derived from a different and sometimes identifiable source. In the following example from *Hamlet,* the authentic speech is given first, and the Bad-Quarto version derived from it is given second; the italicized line interpolated in the authentic text (enclosed in brackets), a line *not* from *Hamlet* but from *Othello*, may have become mingled in the actor's memory with "lend thy serious hearing / To what I shall unfold," an earlier command by the Ghost in the authentic *Hamlet* text but found in the actor's reconstruction only in the altered form shown below in boldface:

(1)
GHOST. I am thy father's spirit,
Doomed for a certain term to walk the night,
And for the day confined to fast in fires,
Till the foul crimes done in my days of nature
Are burnt and purged away.
[To my unfolding, lend thy prosperous ear.]
                        But that I am forbid,
To tell the secrets of my prison-house
I could a tale unfold . . .

(2)
GHOST. I am thy father's spirit, doomed for a time
To walk the night, and all the day
Confined in flaming fire,
Till the foul crimes done in my days of nature
Are purged and burnt away.
HAMLET. Alas poor ghost.
GHOST. Nay pity me not, but **to my unfolding
Lend thy list'ning ear.** But that I am forbid
To tell the secrets of my prison-house,
I would a tale unfold . . .

Stray lines and phrases out of plays by Marlowe and others that found their way into the Bad Quartos of *Henry VI* had once (starting with Malone) been made the basis for suppositions about multiple authorship. Once the surreptitious copies came to be seen as a theatrical class not restricted to Shakespeare, related anomalies, like stray lines of Shakespeare in the mutilated abridgment of Marlowe's *The Massacre at Paris* (itemized in the 1968 edition by H. J. Oliver), fell into place. As Pollard had argued back in 1909, there was no longer any reason to doubt the essential honesty of Hemmings and Condell; or as he put it another way in his Introduction to *Shakespeare's Fight with the Pirates* (1920): "The central idea of the [1915 Sandars Readership in Bibliography] lectures is that the early editions upon which a text of Shakespeare's plays must be built, are a good deal closer to the original manuscripts from his pen than most of the text-builders have allowed."

In his close preparation of the edition that retired the texts of the Pope-to-Johnson era, Capell naturally encountered palpable evidence of Shakespearean autograph manuscripts behind some of the quarto and Folio texts,[15] but his acuity in this regard made too little impression to pierce through the amorphous presumptions of his days about dramatic manuscripts. The opinions about Elizabethan actors, scribes, and printers formulated by Pope during his two years or so of drudgery were the main source for the view put forward by Johnson, in his 1756 *Proposals* (for the edition that he had not yet begun), that Shakespeare's plays generally had been "multiplied by transcript after transcript."

Only in later decades did the actual evidence of the dramatic manuscripts surviving from the theater of Shakespeare's day come to public attention. In 1778 Isaac Reed edited from manuscript Middleton's *The Witch* ("Long since acted by His Majesties Servants at the Black-Friers"), then of interest mainly as the repository of the complete words of two songs whose first lines (only) appear in *Macbeth*. In 1830 Alexander Dyce, one of the ablest editors of the nineteenth century, brought out *Demetrius and Enanthe, Being The Humorous Lieutenant, A Play, by John Fletcher: Published from a Manuscript Dated 1625*. (Both manuscripts have since been re-edited in type-facsimiles by members of the Malone Society to

---

15. 1768 Introduction: "The same matter, and in nearly the same words, is set down twice in some passages; which who sees not to be only a negligence of the poet, and that but one of them ought to have been printed." One of several instances of a "first shot" preserved in the good text of *Romeo and Juliet* occurs in Romeo's final speech. Between the line "And never from this palace of dim night" and the next line in modern editions, "Depart again. Here, here will I remain" the 1599 text prints these four lines: "Depart again, come lie thou in my arm, / Here's to thy health, where e'er thou tumblest in. / Oh true apothecary! / Thy drugs are quick. Thus with a kiss I die." Parts of the four editorially deleted lines reappear in the remaining thirteen lines of the speech (*q.v.*).

preserve and elucidate the evidence of their origins and the characteristics of the professional scribe, Ralph Crane, whose hand they are in and who is now thought to have transcribed the manuscripts from which *The Tempest* and possibly four other Folio plays were printed.) For the newly established Shakespeare Society, Dyce in 1844 edited British Museum MS. Harley 7368, *Sir Thomas More,* into suitably readable form (preserving thereby some readings that have since been lost through deterioration of the manuscript), with the prefatory observation that of its authorship "nothing is known." The conclusion reached between the original Malone Society edition by Greg in 1911 and its supplemented 1961 reprint is that the play was written by (1) Anthony Munday, transcribing a draft of a play of which he was at least part-author, with revisory additions in the hands of (2) Henry Chettle, (3) Thomas Dekker, (4) William Shakespeare in a 147-line scene occupying three leaves, and (5) Thomas Heywood (probable but not certain), along with (as Dyce was aware) notations by an anonymous playhouse book-keeper and a signed note, demanding deletions, by Edmund Tilney, Master of the Revels, at some still undetermined date in the 1590's.

At the beginning of the twentieth century, however, any public understanding of the conditions of Shakespeare's text was still determined by the traditional outlook of editorial pessimism, not yet affected by serious study of the critical playhouse manuscripts. In 1902 Sir Sidney Lee, who since his *Life of Shakespeare* (1898) "had held almost a monopoly of the Shakespeare market in popular esteem" (F. P. Wilson), epitomized the conventional wisdom of that tradition in the Introduction he wrote to accompany the collotype First Folio facsimile from Oxford: "No genuine respect was paid to a dramatic author's original drafts after they reached the playhouse. Scenes and passages were freely erased by the managers . . . Ultimately the dramatist's corrected autograph was copied by the playhouse scrivener; this transcript became the official 'prompt-copy,' and the original was set aside and destroyed, its uses being exhausted." On another page Lee felt free to imagine "a rough copy of the play which had been carelessly transcribed for some subordinate purpose of the playhouse," a conception of protean reliability in supporting almost any chosen line of conjecture.

That Lee had been at least incautious was the message of Greg's criticism in *The Library* of July 1903. "When I asked Pollard whether he would print a review of Lee's introduction he said he would if I would be polite — or words to that effect. I replied that I couldn't undertake to be anything of the kind. This piqued his curiosity, and he gave me a free hand."[16] Greg, then twenty-eight, a Ferdinand among the logs for several years in the Henslowe manuscript documents, wondered "where in the world . . . do we hear of such a person as 'the playhouse scrivener'? We have payments recorded by Henslowe for every possible dramatic expenditure, from building a theatre to sending to the hospital a boy who was injured at a performance, but not a single 'obelus' entered to a copyist. Moreover, we have the best possible evidence that the prompt copy was, in some cases at least, none other than the autograph of the author, for we possess the MS.

16. "W. W. G. (privately communicated)" — p. 78*n.* in F. P. Wilson, "Shakespeare and the 'New Bibliography'," *The Bibliographical Society 1892 - 1942: Studies in Retrospect (1949).*

of Massinger's 'Believe as you list' (Egerton, 2828), which is undoubtedly a prompt copy, containing alterations and corrections, is undoubtedly the authentic acting version submitted to Sir Henry Herbert for license in 1631, and is by the highest expert authority declared to be in the autograph of the author." (The expert alluded to was Sir George Warner, who was responsible for the British Museum's acquisition of the manuscript in 1900 and who had reported the particulars in *The Athenaeum* of 19 January 1901.)

In early 1631 Herbert (Master of the Revels since 1623) read and refused to allow a play by Massinger containing "dangerous matter, as the deposing of Sebastian, king of Portugal." Four months later, at the end of Massinger's revised manuscript (which the King's company book-keeper had also read and augmented with staging notes), he wrote, "This Play, called Beleiue as you liste, may bee acted. this 6. of May. 1631. Henry Herbert." Malone had access to Herbert's Office Book (subsequently lost) and recorded 7 May as the date on which the license-fee for *Believe as you List* was entered, adding (in his *Historical Account of the English Stage*) "This play is lost." One W. R. Chetwood, a prompter at Drury Lane during the era of Colley Cibber, in his later compilation *The British Theatre* (Dublin, 1750) referred to the play as "one I have seen in manuscript, which I am assured was acted, by the proper Quotations &c.," and printed Herbert's licensing note. The manuscript was first brought into print (edited by T. Crofton Croker for the Percy Society) in 1849, but the fact that it "shows all the processes through which the copy passed on the way from the author to the prompter" (as Charles J. Sisson indicated in his 1927

Malone Society edition) was, inevitably, obscure to Croker (hence barely visible through his edition). With the study of English Renaissance autograph literature being then in a very early stage of development, there was little way that the Cambridge editors could have been familiar with this or any other of the few manuscripts then known.

It is hardly attractive to see ourselves as giants by viewing respectable scholars of the past, on whose backs we stand, as pygmies — an anxiety that has surfaced in the commentaries of Shakespeare's editors for over two centuries. But any understanding of *how* the "received text" has come to be received must to some extent depend, in our time, on the recognition that the Cambridge editors came to their textual decisions when editorial experience was restricted mainly to printed books, when the major differences between non-dramatic and theatrical manuscripts (and the resulting differences in prints set up from them) had not yet even been confronted, and when any idea of seriously questioning a century-old editorial tradition of revising Shakespeare's verse-lines into supposedly more regular meters would have been virtually unthinkable. When Greg's great descriptive catalog of *Dramatic Documents from the Elizabethan Playhouses* appeared in 1931, the Malone Society had already published over fifty closely analyzed and annotated editions of early printed and manuscript plays and of documentary records relating to the theatrical circumstances of Shakespeare's time; the paleographic and literary proofs of *Shakespeare's Hand in 'Sir Thomas More'* (1923) had been demonstrated[17] and were among

17. As early as 1871 (in *Notes and Queries*) Richard Simpson gave literary grounds for his belief that a portion of the play was "from

the factors that anyone contemplating a fresh edition of Shakespeare would have to consider; and it had become more difficult for some editors to feel much confidence in the grounds, whatever they were, by which (for example) the Cambridge-Globe text of *Antony and Cleopatra,* Act III, Scene 3 — with thirty-one of its forty-seven verse-lines determined by a Third Folio compositor, Rowe, Pope, Theobald, Capell, and Steevens — might be supposed to represent the intentions of the poet more faithfully than the mixture of verse and prose in the Shakespeare manuscript from which the Folio text derived.

The newly available evidence regarding theatrical manuscripts, as well as the newly disclosed idiosyncrasies of Shakespeare's spelling and handwriting, has had

Shakespeare's head" but was without means to carry a precise case for the manuscript being "from Shakespeare's hand." The known authentic signatures of Shakespeare — the three (and the words "By me") on the will, and the two on documents of 10-11 March 1613 regarding his purchase of a house near the Blackfriars theater (both of the latter constrained within the bounds of a narrow parchment label) — were augmented in 1910 when C. W. Wallace discovered in the Public Record Office the 11 May 1612 deposition dictated by Shakespeare, in response to five questions, in the case of Stephen Bellott vs. Christopher Mountjoy (whose daughter Bellott had married when Shakespeare lodged with the Mountjoys about 1604) and signed by him in a fluent and unconstrained hand. In *Shakespeare's Handwriting* (1916) Sir Edward Maunde Thompson set forth with microscopic lucidity the identity of the hand in the six signatures and the three pages, and the 1923 volume by Thompson, Pollard, Greg, J. Dover Wilson, and R. W. Chambers, *Shakespeare's Hand in 'Sir Thomas More',* set forth the entire range of connections between the scene from *Sir Thomas More* and the rest of the canon that subsequent editorial scholarship has been obliged by the irreversibility of the evidence to take into account. A facsimile, transcript, and modernized text, comprehensively annotated by G. Blakemore Evans, are included in *The Riverside Shakespeare* (1974).

considerable influence on most editors since the 1920's. "There should be no mystery," as Thompson observed, "about the study of handwriting." A back-cover note about F. Scott Fitzgerald on the 1950 Penguin Books (England) edition of *The Great Gatsby* (still found on the 1954 reprint) says that Fitzgerald "gave a name to an age — the 1933 age," and it is reasonable to infer that the note writer's manuscript contained the word *jazz* in lower-case hand-lettering, and that what the compositor set in type was faithful to his own misreading. The best known Shakespearean example among the irregular manuscript spellings of his day is the spelling of *silence* as *scilens* in the *Sir Thomas More* manuscript and in the Good Quarto (1600) of *Henry IV Part 2,* in which, on eighteen occasions, usually in speech prefixes — where there was no context to guide a compositor as to the sound of the writer's intentions — Justice *"Scilens"* is the spelling (so far found nowhere else among the manuscripts and prints of the time). A one-time "great crux" in the 1634 quarto text of *The Two Noble Kinsmen,* hinging on the phrase "sicknes in will / Or wrastling strength in reason" and eliciting futile interpretive struggles of 650-word length from Victorian editors, was resolved in 1965 by recognizing *Or* as a faithful typesetting of Shakespeare's way of spelling *ore (=o'er).*

"Restoring Shakespeare: The Modern Editor's Task," the title of Peter Alexander's widely admired essay in the 1952 issue of the British annual *Shakespeare Survey,* refers to the ongoing restoration of verbal readings in the text of dozens of plays where the Cambridge editors — ignorant of Shakespeare's handwriting and of theatrical manuscripts, working with language that the great Oxford dictionary (begun in 1879) had not yet been compiled to elucidate, quite uninformed about staging at the Globe and Blackfriars, still baffled by the "imperfect" quartos as well as the page-numbering gaps in the Folio — had frequently allowed themselves to depart from the quarto and Folio texts closest to Shakespeare's manuscripts. "Restoring Shakespeare" has also led a few editors, presuming a more than subliminal interest in hearing the speech rhythms of the text, to bring about a change in the rules governing punctuation. The first respectful attempts to sort out and understand such regularities as might be discerned in the early editions were carried out effectively by Alfred Edward Thiselton in the first decade of this century. The result in some recent editions has been a coherent modern punctuation designed to reflect the breath/pause suggestions of the original text ("Boatswain!" "Here master. What cheer?") instead of one with editorial pauses ("Here, master") intended to parse the printed grammar. (The editorial policy decision about one such comma in adopting a system for reprinting thirty-eight plays may implicate thousands of others.) With respect to the broader picture of the text, in his classic summary of what this century has learned about the textual origins of all thirty-six plays of *The Shakespeare First Folio* (1955), Greg brought together and set forth the best organization of the evidence then available; he showed, in most cases quite conclusively, that the great majority of plays were first printed either immediately or (saving the exceptions) at the one remove of an authorized professional transcript from Shakespeare's autograph manuscripts, whether "foul papers"[18] (a finished draft awaiting the annotations and sometimes corrections of a book-keeper) or fair copy. The notoriously variable "office of their care, and pain, to have collected and published" the plays in the Folio at one time elicited only contempt of Hemmings and Condell from later editors. How very far from perfect their supervision might be is visible in exceptional cases like the Folio *Romeo and Juliet,* set from a descendant reprint of the good text from which the leaf containing the Prologue must have become detached and so perfunctorily readied for the printer that the absence escaped detection (until Rowe found another quarto with the Prologue intact and restored it). It can also be seen in their willingness to say in the preface that the reader had been supplied with "all" of Shakespeare's plays although the inclusion (for example) of *Troilus and Cressida,* which is unlisted among the plays in the Folio Catalogue of contents, had probably not yet been secured. But the actions of a few later editors, who have committed the worst outrages upon the text of Shakespeare and then made a point of reviling Hemmings and Condell, should serve as a warning against our regarding their authority, both as company leaders and as veterans of a lifetime of intimacy with Shakespeare, with less than reverence. Nothing in the imperfection of their performance, moreover, argues against the high authority of the

---

18. This term — borrowed from the jargon of Renaissance writers and ubiquitous in present-day textual criticism — is applied by Greg to "a copy representing the play more or less as the author intended it to stand, but not itself clear or tidy enough to serve as a prompt-book." Illustrations of its historical use in manuscripts and books are provided by E. A. J. Honigmann, *The Stability of Shakespeare's Text* (1965), p. 17, and make any more exact definition improbable.

manuscripts they supplied.

In 1935 Penguin Books (England) issued the first ten paperback volumes of the Penguin Shakespeare — never marketed in the United States — which was edited (initially on the recommendation of Harley Granville-Barker) by G. B. Harrison and completed in 1959 (with the final volume, *The Narrative Poems*, containing an epilogue by Harrison describing the inception and planning of the series). To American eyes it is the most unusual modern-spelling edition of Shakespeare (the poems and thirty-seven plays) that has been published to date, since in general it abandons the Cambridge-Globe metrical reorganization in favor of the line arrangement in the basic quarto and Folio texts. The passage below from *Julius Caesar*, Act I, Scene 3 should illustrate the difference:

> CASSIUS: You are dull, Casca,
> And those sparks of life, that should be in a Roman,
> You do want, or else you use not.
> You look pale, and gaze, and put on fear,
> And cast yourself in wonder,
> To see the strange impatience of the heavens . . .

These lines, thus printed, swarming with vital cues to pauses and emphasis, a storehouse of acting information on the sound and weight and feel of the voices, in 1709 were turned into neurotic pentameter by the leading playwright in town:

> CASSIUS: You are dull, Casca, and those sparks of life
> That should be in a Roman you do want,
> Or else you use not. You look pale, and gaze,
> And put on fear, and cast yourself in wonder, . . .

The Folio text of *Julius Caesar* is by common editorial consent the best printed and most trouble-free of all

Shakespeare first editions. Given that Rowe's rearrangement was accepted and numbered by the Cambridge editors and has thereby been admitted to most modern editions, it should be observed that the narrow width of a Folio column, sometimes adduced as a reason for a compositor producing "mislineation," could not have affected these lines of Cassius, since the second line in the authentic text

> And those sparks of life, that should be in a Roman,

is longer than any of the lines in Rowe's reconstruction. Compositors, moreover, seem to have been far less poetical than the eighteenth-century editors, and if we charitably assume that Rowe actually thought he was reconstructing what Shakespeare had originally written, we have a commensurately greater problem on our hands in trying to explain why the compositor took such odd and special pains to confound the manuscript. Many Folio lines that are not pentameter length — from Murullus's "Be gone!" in his first long speech of the play's opening scene to the lines "Unto this monstrous state" and "Most like this dreadful night" later in this same speech by Cassius to Casca — were approved and licensed by the Cambridge-Globe editors and thereby survive in all modern editions. What Harrison did in his English Penguin Shakespeare was, in effect, to clean up the Augean stables of eighteenth-century metrical revision, thereby providing a modern text that was apt to be metrically closer than the Cambridge-Globe to Shakespeare's own conscious choice by any credible calculation of probability.

In 1948 Harcourt, Brace and Company (New York), later the publisher of Harrison's autobiographical *Profession of English* (1962) and others of his books, brought out an edition of *Shakespeare: Major Plays and the Sonnets* "Edited by G. B. Harrison, University of Michigan," in which the Preface begins as follows:

> This edition of twenty-three of Shakespeare's plays, with the sonnets, has been produced for college students in the hope that it will help them to understand, appreciate, and enjoy the plays for themselves. It is not intended for the scholar, who is amply served elsewhere.
>
> The choice of a text gave considerable difficulty. When the volume was first planned there was hot controversy whether to use the familiar Globe text or to print a text which closely followed the original quarto or Folio, on the lines of my Penguin Shakespeares. It was therefore agreed to submit the problem to a plebiscite of professors and to abide by their judgment. The vote was decidedly in favor of the Globe . . .

Unfortunately no more detailed information has ever been made public regarding the special judgment by which students were mandated to continue receiving the familiar if unreliable Globe text while scholars, privy perhaps to the secrets of some inner professional fiefdoms, were to be considered apart from the horde of youth in the swelling textbook marketplace.

While continuing to edit new Shakespeare titles along authentic lines for Penguin Books in England, Harrison also contributed "A Note on *Coriolanus*" to the Folger Shakespeare Library *Joseph Quincy Adams Memorial Studies* (1948) in which, after spending one page on newly observed evidence favoring a late-1609 date for *Coriolanus*, he allowed himself twelve pages for an effort to commend his fellow scholars' patient attention to several passages in *Coriolanus, Antony and Cleopatra, Macbeth,* and other plays so that they might experience the ways Pope and other editors had "proceeded to set Shakespeare right in his prosody; it is a sign of the docility of editors that their 'improvements' have been accepted without question ever since." In his 1949 review of textual studies among "The Year's Contributions to Shakespearian Study" in *Shakespeare Survey,* James G. McManaway (then editor of *Shakespeare Quarterly*) treated the Harrison essay in relation to another 1948 publication, an unusual book written by a German poet for an English-language audience:

> A fresh approach to some of the textual problems in Shakespeare is found in *Shakespeare's Producing Hand.* Certain technicalities of versification, rhythm, diction, and punctuation that are rarely commented on by Shakespearians have forced themselves upon the attention of the author, Richard Flatter, while he has been engaged in transcribing and translating into German the *Sonnets* and eighteen of the plays. And though there will be disagreement about some of the details, Flatter is sound enough in his insistence upon the restoration of much of the original lineation and punctuation that was 'improved' by the eighteenth-century editors . . .
> In "A Note on Coriolanus," G. B. Harrison employs similar methods to show how modern editions sacrifice much of the dramatic value of certain scenes by retaining the regularized lineation of the early editors and thus obscuring Shakespeare's revelation of character and mood by his fluent accommodation of the verse to the passions of his *dramatis personae.* "The result," for readers who have not ready access to facsimiles of the Quartos and the Folio, "is to destroy most of Shakespeare's subtle touches; to abolish the pauses, the silences, and the rushes . . . The gain is that with a little forcing we can now recite [the] speeches to the accompaniment of that inspiring instrument — the metronome."

Actually the metrical footprints of the early editors, as the scene between Cleopatra and the Messenger alone may suffice to indicate, do not really measure up even with respect to metronomic regularity, and if some gain is to be located anywhere it is not likely to be a gain for the reader, the actor, the poet, or the student — only for the traditional vested interests of poorly advised publishers and a number of acquiescent or indifferent professors of English.

Brief as it is, the scene that Shakespeare contributed to the chronicle play about Sir Thomas More must figure importantly in any consideration of his manuscript routine. An unruly mob has been whipped up by a broker named John Lincoln ("he that will not see . . . butter at a levenpence a pound, . . . list to me") and wants London rid of alien workers who are depriving natives of jobs and are driving up prices. After the Mayor and other officials try without success, More (then a Sheriff) begins the process of calming the mob.

> *More.* You that have voice and credit with the number,
> Command them to a stillness.
> *Lincoln.* A plague on them, they will not hold their peace. The dev'l cannot rule them.
> *More.* Then what a rough and riotous charge have you
> To lead those that the dev'l cannot rule. —
> Good masters, hear me speak.

(One sidelight on the first line above — visible in the actual-size facsimile in *Shakespeare's Handwriting* or the reduced ones in *Shakespeare Survey 2* [1949] and *The Riverside Shakespeare* — is that Shakespeare seems to have started to write *multitude* and then, whether for metrical or other reasons, deleted *Mu* and wrote *number*.) Between the passage above and the close of the scene there are thirteen speeches, similarly arranged, five of them in verse by More (ranging in length from four lines up to forty-three lines with an interlineated half-line addition) and eight others (none over two lines) in prose by spokesmen for the commons. The opening and closing lines of the verse speeches are notable, as a metrical class, for the high number of departures from a pentameter norm. One of the opening and three of the closing lines ("Would feed on one another"; "You were in arms 'gainst God"; "Nay certainly you are"; "If you so seek it"), like the two closing verse-lines above, come next to speeches in prose and are thus left without any part-lines to complement their meter. Since the same practice is evident throughout almost all the quarto and Folio texts, the chances are very slim indeed that typographical hemistichs like

                                                   Three in Egypt
Cannot make better note.

bear any conceivable relation to what Shakespeare had in mind when he wrote an integrated line. (It should be borne in mind that no one editor alone created these sclerotic meters; they may have been sired by Pope and Capell, but they were finally delivered by Steevens out of white space.) Apart from the interpolated half line, all but a few of the remaining seventy-five verse lines in the five speeches are ten- or eleven-syllable pentameters. The exceptions are a few alexandrines and one line of fourteen syllables ("To slip him like a hound; alas, alas, say now the King") that is sufficient to show that the long lines from the Gardener's speech in *Richard II* do not require Capell's metrical surgery any more than the sense requires his redundant "We." Prose is also clear enough in the three pages; speech prefixes appear in the left quarter of the page (marked by a fold) normally reserved for them, and the dialogue, beginning at the quarter-fold, usually extends through the second and third quarters if it is in verse and into the fourth if it is prose. The spacing is more distinctive to the eye in an eight-inch-wide manuscript leaf than in one of the double columns of the Folio and is certainly distinct enough to allow the presumption that the Folio compositor of *Antony and Cleopatra,* Act III, Scene 3 was reading prose in the manuscript wherever he set prose into type.

In the century following the Cambridge-Globe Shakespeare the advances made by dedicated scholars in understanding the underlying theatrical and printing conditions of Shakespeare's text have been massively documented and widely publicized, and the verbal fidelity of present-day editions of Shakespeare has been substantially improved. Respectful consideration of the seemingly narrow issue of line arrangement, meanwhile, has been comparatively limited, and the perceptions and performances by Harrison, Flatter, McManaway, and others have not, as yet, much affected the international Shakespeare industry. A few established editors, like M. R. Ridley in the 1954 New Arden edition of *Antony and Cleopatra,* have explicitly espoused a traditional editorial conviction — mainly confined for some reason to editors of Shakespeare's plays — that the poet's versification is entirely subject to the jurisdiction of the editor's ear, which in his case exactly agrees in Act III, Scene 3 with all the variegated decisions about verse and prose arrived at between 1663 and 1864 wherever they contradict the evidence in the Folio. A few editors of individual plays in serial editions have shown more sensitivity to the early texts and less docility to the editorial tradition. A 1954 revision by Eugene M. Waith of the Yale Shakespeare *Macbeth* restores some of the Folio line arrangement on the fair assumption that the cadences intended by Shakespeare in (for example) the lines about Cawdor

> Nothing in his life became him,
> Like the leaving it. He died,
> As one that had been studied in his death . . .

were more likely to be found in this Folio arrangement than in Pope's attempt to reformulate them according to the standards of an altered literary ideal. Maynard Mack, distinguished contributor to the Twickenham Edition of Pope and an authoritative student of Pope's versification, made a point of eliminating all traces of Pope's versification from Shakespeare's play when he edited *Henry IV Part 1* (1965) for the Signet Classic Shakespeare, liberating Shakespeare's prose from its Augustan metrical corset (cf. note 13 above) and providing readers with what is still rare in modern editions of Shakespeare — credible assurance that the neo-classic scrim of metrical corruption has in fact been removed.

The handsomely designed little volumes in Harrison's Penguin Shakespeare series are only lightly annotated and they also lack any printed numbering of the lines, rendering them inconvenient for reference and for some kinds of scholastic use; whether for these or other reasons the American branch of Penguin Books in 1956 began to bring out a different series in the United States, the Pelican Shakespeare, under the general editorship of Alfred Harbage. The Pelican texts improve upon mistaken or misleading scene divisions of the Cambridge-Globe text but in general follow without modification or explanation the Cambridge line arrangements. The Harrison texts were often reprinted in England well into the 1960's (and have also been printed in the United States to accompany the Shakespeare Recording Society audio recordings of the plays published by Caedmon Records), but in 1967 they began to be replaced by the individually edited New Penguin series, still in progress and generally in accord with the Cambridge lines. Harrison's essentially Shakespeare-lined text is thus gradually disappearing from the world market. More recently *The Riverside Shakespeare,* whose line numbering for all thirty-eight plays and *Sir Thomas More* governs the line references in the recent *Harvard Concordance to Shakespeare,* appeared with a Publisher's Preface stating that

> the book has been designed with the general reader, the student, and the scholar equally in mind.
>
> The plan of the volume was ambitious from the start. The central spire of its accomplishment is a completely re-edited text, generally modern in its spelling and punctuation, yet sensitively reflecting the rhythms and modulations of the Elizabethan voice. This text and its appurtenances, including full textual notes and a history of Shakespeare textual scholarship and editing, is the sole work of G. Blakemore Evans of Harvard University, and will, we believe, stand as a model for generations to come.

The Riverside textual notes in their fullness identify changes of prose to verse and verse to prose but are quite devoid of information on the innumerable line rearrangements. As for the "completely re-edited text," in Act III, Scene 3 of *Antony and Cleopatra* the only difference from the lineation of the Cambridge text is that "Octavia" has been moved back from line 8 to line 7. Since 1968, when the *Norton Facsimile* of the First Folio was published with a copyrighted "Through Line Numbering" system (one that ignores scene division and runs into four digits) printed in the margins, interested scholars have been able to escape the Cambridge reference system in their writing for learned journals. But modern-spelling editions for the general public and for students are mostly still bound to the old editorial rearrangements, and anyone with a keen interest in Shakespeare's rhythms in their authoritative form must look for them elsewhere.[19]

In their preface Hemmings and Condell said that the texts of the plays in the Folio were "absolute in their numbers." Special exceptions (like *Timon of Athens*) and occasional printing errors in the Folio forbid anyone from ever taking their statement quite literally. Where, for example, the printer failed to "cast off" — measure out — the manuscript properly, as on page 192 of the Comedies section, he might deliberately waste white space around headings to fill out the page and even take an entire brief scene that is clearly prose — in this instance Act II, Scene 6 of *As You Like It* — and set it extremely loosely as verse. In comparison with the Rowe-to-Wright editorial tradition of dismembered and re-composed meters, however, the texts that Hemmings and Condell printed might well be called absolute in their numbers. The departures from them certainly bring no gain to any form of understanding. Near the end of Act II, Scene 3 of *Macbeth,* the rhythmic connectedness of the consecutive speeches between the two princes in their first private conversation after their father's murder is apparent enough in the Folio arrangement:

> MALCOLM: What will you do?
>   Let's not consort with them.
>   To show an unfelt sorrow is an office
>   Which the false man does easy.
>   I'll to England.
> DONALBAIN: To Ireland I.

19. The Folio arrangement of a passage from *The Tempest* that might be of interest to an actor studying the lines of Caliban is presented, by way of illustration, in the Afterword.

> Our separated fortune shall keep us both the safer.
> Where we are, there's daggers in men's smiles;
> The near in blood, the nearer bloody.

On the other hand, the rhythms are muddled, along with much else of spoken phrase-length interest, by the pointless compression of these nine lines into the seven peculiarly unnatural pentameters any reader may find in almost any modern edition:

> MALCOLM: What will you do? Let's not consort with them.
> To show an unfelt sorrow is an office
> Which the false man does easy. I'll to England.
> DONALBAIN: To Ireland I. Our separated fortune
> Shall keep us both the safer. Where we are,
> There's daggers in men's smiles; the near in blood,
> The nearer bloody.

The chief obstacle to getting a trustworthy modern text may just possibly consist in some such mindless element as the white spaces inserted by Steevens, whom many of his editorial successors have regarded as infamous on other grounds, into the rest of the accumulated eighteenth-century metrical mishmash. Ultimate authority for these white spaces is invisible, but if the literary professions still require the clear assessment of responsibility then Steevens certainly deserves the credit for this protean interference with Shakespeare's verse. If the white spaces are abandoned as they were in Harrison's Penguin text (and as they have been in another more recent selected edition)[20] it might be possible to get a complete edition of Shakespeare less vulnerable to charges of editorial negligence or misrepresentation.

20. The Hayden Shakespeare Series (New York, 1973), edited by Maynard Mack and Robert W. Boynton, which so far includes *Hamlet*, *Macbeth*, *Julius Caesar*, and *Henry IV Part 1*.

The issue of editorial verse is less easily ignored than in the past. The text of the 1976 New Arden edition of *Coriolanus*, like most others, uses the same line arrangements that were accepted by the Cambridge editors; but the New Arden editor, Philip Brockbank, offers some commentary on these arrangements in the twelve-page section of his 89-page Introduction that is devoted to "Lineation": "Since the beginning of the eighteenth century editorial tradition has intervened in more than a hundred and twenty passages to make adjustments affecting over three hundred line-divisions in the edited text." By way of illustration Brockbank singles out "the largest single group of adjustments of the Folio lineation in modern texts (about forty)" as that which

consists of transitions between speeches, often short ones and sometimes mixing verse and prose. Attempts to regularize transitions often affect the lines that follow, and it would be rash to claim that anything resembling the regularized text actually stood in the copy. For instance, II.i.234-41 F reads,

Toth' people, begge their stinking Breaths.
Scicin. 'Tis right.
Brutus. It was his word:
Oh he would misse it, rather then carry it,
But by the suite of the Gentry to him,
And the desire of the Nobles.
Scicin. I wish no better, then haue him hold that purpose,
and to put it in execution.
Brutus. 'Tis most like he will.
Scicin. It shall be to him then, as our good wills; a sure destruction.

Attempts at regularization by Steevens, Pope, and Rowe yield,
To th'people, beg their stinking breaths.
Sic. 'Tis right.
Bru. It was his word. Oh, he would miss it rather
Than carry it but by the suit of the gentry to him
And the desire of the nobles.

66

> *Bru.*   I wish no better
> Than have him hold that purpose, and to put it
> In execution.
> *Bru.*   'Tis most like he will.
> *Sic.* It shall be to him then, as our good wills,
> A sure destruction.

Conceding that editorial lines like "Than carry it but by the suit of the gentry to him" may be regarded as "infelicities" with respect to meter, and speculating that Shakespeare "hesitated between verse and prose," Brockbank (whose own text of course follows the edited version exactly) then observes: "The edited version cannot here be justified either as an approximation to copy or as a recovery of the author's intention; it is rather an interpretation of an intention imperfectly achieved." The revisions that were locked into place by the Cambridge editors, a pastiche of disparate changes stemming from misunderstandings that span centuries of our literary history, are evidently now to be provided with a new justification, in the face of admittedly contradictory evidence, as the fulfillment of "an interpretation of an intention imperfectly achieved"!

That editors are obliged to respect the readings of the original texts or else justify their alterations case by case is a basic principle in all state-of-the-art modern editing. In the verbal treatment of Shakespeare's text this principle is more or less generally adhered to, but in the metrical custom of most editions we find instead a consistent adherence only to the assorted sophistications by "the many able and learned Editors" to whom Clark, Glover, and Wright deferred when they initiated the Cambridge-Globe line-numbering system. When Pope conflated the good and bad texts of *Henry V* and tidied up the meters, he was acting on the cloudiest assumptions about the original texts, from which it took generations for scholars to liberate themselves. The peculiar metrical configurations that evolved into the Cambridge text — of which the Messenger's scene from *Antony and Cleopatra* affords a concise illustration, and in which the ghost of Steevens haunts almost every echelon-arranged line in the canon — no more deserves to be maintained in common use than Pope's adaptation of *Henry V*. A new complete edition along authentic lines, following the general precedent of Harrison's Penguin text (accompanied by suitable annotation, of course, and furnished with a proper new act-scene-line-numbering scale) would bring the reading public much closer to Shakespeare's own rhythmic notation and editorial practitioners much closer to their professed goals.

Afterword

The metrical issue that emerges from this editorial history of Shakespeare's text ought perhaps to be glanced at from a number of wider (or at any rate different) perspectives. With regard to the argument that a new complete edition of Shakespeare is needed, for example, it has to be understood that the merit of any new edition would depend on the quality of its annotation and commentary almost as much as on the quality of its text, and that the quality of its text would obviously depend on its treatment of variant verbal readings as well as on its metrical form. The argument in these pages is simply that the most broadly extensive improvement that might be made in the text of any new edition would be the comprehensive shift from one metrical form (the collective neo-classical revision that was standardized by the Cambridge-Globe edition and that is still preserved a century later in the Riverside edition) to the alternative form derived from the original textual sources (as in the Penguin and Hayden editions).

With regard to the reader experiencing the play in the "theater of the mind," the result would be a better dramatic apprehension of the sounds and pauses of particular speeches. For example, in *Coriolanus,* Act I, Scene 9 (after Corioles has fallen), Martius (in his first speech in the scene, arranged here as in the Folio) rejects the praise of Cominius and Titus Lartius in these lines:

> I have done as you have done, that's what I can;
> Induced as you have been, that's for my country.

The clarity of the speech rhythm is helped by the presence of two clauses and two strong rests in each of two almost parallel lines. It is not helped, and may not even be immediately evident, in the rearrangement going back to Hanmer that editors continue to print:

>   I have done
> As you have done, that's what I can; induced
> As you have been, that's for my country.[21]

(It might be of potential critical value if an authentically lined new edition were to reprint in an appendix a selection of the more radical editorial rearrangements, each example serving as a foil to set off the superiority of the original rhythms.) At a turning point in the dialogue between Ulysses and Achilles in *Troilus and Cressida,* Act III, Scene 3 (after the Grecian lords on Ulysses' advice have snubbed Achilles and Ulysses has held up Ajax as a threat to his reputation), Achilles' brief response to Ulysses shows the first signs that his lesson is taking hold — in four end-stopped lines, each as separate in thought as in sound:

---

21. Lines 17-19 (Cambridge or Riverside text). The original text of the entire scene (Folio Tragedies, p. 7) is worth comparing with the edited text as it had been progressively sophisticated by Pope, Hanmer, Steevens, and others. Hanmer's line 19 contained an insertion of his own to make a pentameter:
> As you have also been, that's for my country.

Later editors deleted the insertion but kept the Hanmer line. Their cumulative metrical inconsistencies (filling out some short lines, leaving others alone, arranging new ones of their own) preclude any defense of the resulting Cambridge/Riverside readings on specifically metrical grounds, given the metrical dilettantism out of which they originated.

Among the many lines spoken in this scene whose original emphases are obscured by editors, of particular note is the speech in which Cominius replies to Martius, beginning:
> You shall not be the grave of your deserving,
> Rome must know the value of her own . . .

ULYSSES: . . . even already
  They clap the lubber Ajax on the shoulder,
  As if his foot were on brave Hector's breast,
  And great Troy shrieking.
ACHILLES: I do believe it.
  For they passed by me, as misers do by beggars,
  Neither gave to me good word, nor look.
  What, are my deeds forgot?

These sullen deliberations by Achilles (lined above as in the 1609 and 1623 texts) are jumbled by later editors into three lines that were first run together by Capell:

ACHILLES: I do believe it. For they passed by me,
  As misers do by beggars, neither gave to me
  Good word, nor look. What, are my deeds forgot?

Rearranging words on a page may be thought to have little effect on their meaning. However, the difference between the original and the rearranged texts (the damage done by the latter to the former) has to do with a continuous stream of subtle relationships between sound and sense that, even when they don't rise above the threshold of consciousness, impinge on the mind of any reader attentive to variations of stress and pause in dramatic speech. They may only rarely become the subject of conscious critical attention, but their influence on the quality of reading is undeniable.

It might also be worth considering the utility of a new edition from the pragmatic viewpoint of the actor, since each play was, after all, first composed for live performance. That reading a play is somewhat like reading a musical score (the analogy popularized by Granville-Barker) has always been well appreciated among members of the theatrical profession: "Comedies are writ to be spoken, not read," John Marston insisted in 1606, "remember the life of these things consists in action..."[22]

It is, in any case, reasonable to suppose that the significance of different line arrangements ought to be related to their possible effects on dramatic and poetic values in performance. One example to illustrate this point, to suggest how even very small and widely scattered metrical changes may affect theatrical results, is an episode from Act II, Scene 2 of *The Tempest* that occupies 114 lines in the original Folio text.

The episode centers on Caliban, "whose life rests much in the actor's voice." His very first encounter with the audience, in Act I, Scene 2, had been as a decidedly surly disembodied offstage voice refusing a summons from Prospero merely to appear: "There's wood enough within." Act II, Scene 2 opens to a noise of nearby thunder with Caliban coming on stage alone, carrying a burden of logs and cursing Prospero. When Trinculo enters, Caliban takes him to be a spirit sent by Prospero "to torment me / For bringing wood in slowly"; and when Stephano enters, drinking and singing, Caliban (looking up at him from beneath the gaberdine under which he and Trinculo are now lying down) starts out by making the same mistake again. Throughout the entire passage (printed here in a form that follows the Folio text exactly with respect to verse/prose distinctions) Caliban is speaking in prose, apart from a single line of verse near the end.

    CALIBAN: Do not torment me. Oh!
    STEPHANO: What's the matter?
        Have we devils here?

22. "To my equal reader," *The Fawn,* ed. Gerald A. Smith (1965), p. 5. Cf. p. 3: "If any shall wonder why I print a comedy, whose life rests much in the actor's voice, let such know that it cannot avoid publishing. Let it therefore stand with good excuse, that I have been my own setter out."

Do you put tricks upon's with savages, and men of Ind, ha? I have not 'scaped drowning, to be afeard now of your four legs. For it hath been said, as proper a man as ever went on four legs cannot make him give ground. And it shall be said so again, while Stephano breathes at' nostrils.

CALIBAN: The spirit torments me. Oh!

STEPHANO: This is some monster of the isle, with four legs, who hath got, as I take it, an ague. Where the devil should he learn our language? I will give him some relief, if it be but for that. If I can recover him, and keep him tame, and get to Naples with him, he's a present for any emperor that ever trod on neat's-leather.

CALIBAN: Do not torment me prithee. I'll bring my wood home faster.

STEPHANO: He's in his fit now, and does not talk after the wisest. He shall taste of my bottle. If he have never drunk wine afore, it will go near to remove his fit. If I can recover him, and keep him tame, I will not take too much for him; he shall pay for him that hath him, and that soundly.

CALIBAN: Thou dost me yet but little hurt; thou wilt anon, I know it by thy trembling. Now Prosper works upon thee.

STEPHANO: Come on your ways. Open your mouth. Here is that which will give language to you, cat. Open your mouth; this will shake your shaking, I can tell you, and that soundly. You cannot tell who's your friend; open your chaps again.

TRINCULO: I should know that voice.

It should be —

But he is drowned, and these are devils. Oh defend me!

STEPHANO: Four legs and two voices — a most delicate monster. His forward voice now is to speak well of his friend; his backward voice is to utter foul speeches, and to detract. If all the wine in my bottle will recover him, I will help his ague. Come. Amen, I will pour some in thy other mouth.

TRINCULO: Stephano.

STEPHANO: Doth thy other mouth call me? Mercy, mercy! This is a devil, and no monster; I will leave him, I have no long spoon.

TRINCULO: Stephano. If thou beest Stephano, touch me, and speak to me. For I am Trinculo — be not afeard — thy good friend Trinculo.

STEPHANO: If thou beest Trinculo, come forth. I'll pull thee by the lesser legs. If any be Trinculo's legs, these are they.*[Pulls him out by the legs.]* Thou art very Trinculo indeed. How cam'st thou to be the siege of this moon-calf? Can he vent Trinculos?

TRINCULO: I took him to be killed with a thunder-stroke. But art thou not drowned, Stephano? I hope now thou art not drowned. Is the storm overblown? I hid me under the dead moon-calf's gaberdine, for fear of the storm. And art thou living, Stephano? Oh Stephano, two Neapolitans 'scaped!

STEPHANO: Prithee do not turn me about, my stomach is not constant.

CALIBAN: These be fine things, and if they be not sprites. That's a brave god, and bears celestial liquor. I will kneel to him.

STEPHANO: How didst thou 'scape?

How cam'st thou hither?

Swear by this bottle how thou cam'st hither. I escaped upon a butt of sack, which the sailors heaved overboard, by this bottle which I made of the bark of a tree, with mine own hands, since I was cast ashore.

CALIBAN: I'll swear upon that bottle to be thy true subject, for the liquor is not earthly.

STEPHANO: Here. Swear then how thou escapedst.

TRINCULO: Swum ashore, man, like a duck. I can swim like a duck, I'll be sworn.

STEPHANO: Here, kiss the book. *[Gives him the bottle.]* Though thou canst swim like a duck, thou art made like a goose.

TRINCULO: Oh Stephano, hast any more of this?

STEPHANO: The whole butt, man; my cellar is in a rock by the sea-side, where my wine is hid.

How now moon-calf, how does thine ague?

CALIBAN: Hast thou not dropped from heaven?

STEPHANO: Out o' the moon I do assure thee. I was the man-i'-the-moon, when time was.

CALIBAN: I have seen thee in her. And I do adore thee. My mistress showed me thee, and thy dog, and thy bush.

STEPHANO: Come, swear to that. Kiss the book. I will furnish it anon with new contents. Swear.

TRINCULO: By this good light, this is a very shallow monster.

I afeard of him? A very weak monster.
The man-i'-the-moon?
A most poor credulous monster — *[Caliban drinks again.]*
Well drawn monster, in good sooth.
CALIBAN: I'll show thee every fertile inch o' th' island. And I will kiss thy foot. I prithee be my god.
TRINCULO: By this light, a most perfidious and drunken monster. When's god's asleep he'll rob his bottle.
CALIBAN: I'll kiss thy foot. I'll swear myself thy subject.
STEPHANO: Come on then. Down and swear.
TRINCULO: I shall laugh myself to death at this puppy-headed monster. A most scurvy monster. I could find in my heart to beat him —
STEPHANO: Come, kiss.
TRINCULO: — but that the poor monster's in drink.
An abominable monster.
CALIBAN: I'll show thee the best springs. I'll pluck thee berries. I'll fish for thee, and get thee wood enough.
A plague upon the tyrant that I serve!
I'll bear him no more sticks, but follow thee, thou wondrous man.

Caliban's slavish fear in his earlier speeches disappears during the passage in which he has his first experience of intoxication and comes around, virtually transfigured in the eyes and ears of an audience attending the play for the first time, to his radiant vision of Stephano as his liberator, "thou wondrous man." All of his declarations to Stephano ("I prithee be my god . . . I'll kiss thy foot . . . I'll pluck thee berries. I'll fish for thee, and get thee wood enough . . . ") are expressed through fevered speeches in prose, for Caliban is suffused not only with alcohol but with a new mode of dedicated servility toward his brave new god. He suddenly shifts away from prose, however, right after promising Stephano to "get thee wood enough," for a one-line pentameter curse on Prospero ("A plague upon the tyrant that I serve!"), where the shift in rhythm underlines the radical shift in tone.

A good actor studying the part of Caliban may or may not absolutely need the exact prose/verse guidance of the Folio text to grasp the rhythmic distinction between his enthusiastic prose declarations to Stephano and the altered sound of the line in which he calls down a plague on Prospero. Still, neither he nor any other reader ought to have such a distinction obscured or confused by a text that follows Pope in printing the final speech as five consecutive lines of verse. Most current editions also follow the Cambridge-Globe precedent in printing one other speech by Caliban in this episode (beginning at "These be fine things . . . " and ending with "I will kneel to him.") as three lines of Johnson-arranged verse but leaving the rest as prose. Other neo-classical editors have sometimes converted still more of these speeches by Caliban into variant verse arrangements. But whether the number of lines converted by editors is large or small, the quality of many fine details in the actor's performance as Caliban is apt to be at risk if the actor regards his text as a vocal score in a presumably authoritative poetic notation. The best available evidence of the spoken rhythms, the excellent and carefully printed Folio text, has been trivially but fatally contaminated.

Although there are fewer verbal emendations in modern editions of *The Tempest* than in almost any other play in the canon, editorial verse/prose rearrangements have been introduced in some sixty passages (scattered throughout the text) of two to six lines each, and they are noteworthy for their inconsistency. In the episode above, the two speeches by Caliban that editors routinely turn into verse both conclude with irregular short lines;

"I will kneel to him" was made a single line by Johnson, and "Thou wondrous man" by Pope. But with the seven speeches by Stephano and Trinculo in the same episode that contain one to three short lines in the Folio text, the common practice of editors since Pope has been to eliminate them entirely (consolidating them with the prose in each of the seven speeches), possibly — one can only guess — because they are not of pentameter length. These changes are no help to the actor. Stephano, Alonzo's butler, whose own royal imaginings are stirred up in this scene, may not be steady on his feet but is not therefore any the less self-assured: he has a propensity for lofty pronouncements ("it hath been said . . . And it shall be said . . ."). An actor studying the role might well wish to make use of the phrase-length and pause suggestions of the Folio text as cues for vocal emphasis in shaping his performance. It is, in any case, those who would defend a text incorporating the editorial revisions on whom the onus of proof would appear to rest, and the inconsistency of editors who reject the short lines of the Folio while embracing those of Pope and Johnson, without any discernible editorial principle, argues that the arrangements in the original text are more deserving of the actor's attention and respect.

Bibliography

A. Post-1700 Editions of Shakespeare Cited

The Works of Mr. William Shakespear. Revis'd and corrected, with an account of the life and writings of the author. Edited by Nicholas Rowe. 6 vols. London, 1709.

The Works of Shakespear. Collated and corrected by the former editions. Edited by Alexander Pope. 6 vols. London, 1725.

The Works of Shakespeare. Collated with the oldest copies and corrected; with notes, explanatory and critical. Edited by Lewis Theobald. 7 vols. London, 1733.

The Works of Shakespear. Carefully revised and corrected. Edited by Sir Thomas Hanmer. 6 vols. Oxford, 1744.

The Works of Shakespear. The genuine text (collated with all the former editions, and then corrected and emended) is here settled; being restored from the blunders of the first editors and the interpolations of the two last; with a comment and notes, critical and explanatory, by Mr. Pope and Mr. Warburton. Edited by William Warburton. 8 vols. London, 1747.

The Plays of William Shakespeare. With the corrections and illustrations of various commentators, to which are added notes. Edited by Samuel Johnson. 8 vols. London, 1765.

*Mr. William Shakespeare his Comedies, Histories, and Tragedies, set out by himself in quarto, or by the players his fellows in folio, and now faithfully republish'd with an introduction. Whereunto will be added, in some other volumes, notes, critical and explanatory, and a body of various readings. Edited by Edward Capell. 10 vols. London, 1768.

The Plays of William Shakespeare. With the corrections and illustrations of various commentators; to which are added notes by Samuel Johnson and George Steevens. Edited by Johnson and Steevens. 10 vols. London, 1773.

The Plays of William Shakspeare . . . Notes by Samuel Johnson and George Steevens. Second edition, revised and augmented. Edited by Johnson and Steevens. 10 vols. London, 1778.

Supplement to the Edition of Shakspeare's Plays Published in 1778 by Samuel Johnson and George Steevens. Edited by Edmond Malone. 2 vols. London, 1780.

The Plays of William Shakspeare . . . Notes by Samuel Johnson and George Steevens. Third edition, revised and augmented by the Editor of Dodsley's Collection of Old Plays. Edited by Isaac Reed. 10 vols. London, 1785.

The Plays and Poems of William Shakspeare. Collated verbatim with the most authentick copies, and revised; with the corrections and illustrations of various commentators; to which are added an Essay on the Chronological Order of his Plays; an Essay relative to Shakspeare and Jonson; a Dissertation on the Three Parts of King Henry VI; an Historical Account of the English Stage; and notes. Edited by Malone. 10 vols. London, 1790.

The Plays of William Shakspeare . . . Notes by Samuel Johnson and George Steevens. Fourth edition, revised and augmented (with a glossarial index). Edited by

Steevens. 15 vols. London, 1793.

The Plays of William Shakspeare . . . Notes by Samuel Johnson and George Steevens. Fifth edition. Edited by Reed. 21 vols. London, 1803.

The Plays of William Shakspeare . . . Notes by Samuel Johnson and George Steevens. Sixth Edition. Edited by Reed. 21 vols. London, 1813.

The Plays and Poems of William Shakspeare. With the corrections and illustrations of various commentators; comprehending a Life of the Poet, and an Enlarged History of the Stage by the late Edmond Malone. Edited by Malone and James Boswell. 21 vols. London, 1821.

The First Edition of the Tragedy of Hamlet . . . 1603. Reprinted . . . for Payne and Foss. London, 1825.

Sir Thomas More, a Play. Edited by Alexander Dyce. (Shakespeare Society, vol. 23.) London, 1844.

Hamlet. Facsimile of 1603 Quarto. Supervised by J. Payne Collier. London, 1858.

The Works of William Shakespeare. Edited by William George Clark, John Glover, and William Aldis Wright. 9 vols. Cambridge, 1863-66. (Second edition, 1891-93.)

Hamlet. Facsimile of 1603 Quarto. Supervised by William Griggs; Foreword by Frederick J. Furnivall. London, 1880.

Shakespeares Comedies, Histories, & Tragedies. Facsimile of the First Folio edition, 1623. Introduction by Sidney Lee. Oxford, 1902.

The Book of Sir Thomas More. Edited by W. W. Greg. (Malone Society.) Oxford, 1911. (Reprinted, with Supplement by Harold Jenkins, 1961.)

The Penguin Shakespeare. Edited by G. B. Harrison. 37 vols. Harmondsworth, 1935-59.

Major Plays and the Sonnets. Edited by G. B. Harrison. New York, 1948.

Antony and Cleopatra. Edited by M. R. Ridley. (The Arden Shakespeare.) London, 1954.

Macbeth. Edited by Eugene M. Waith. (The Yale Shakespeare.) New Haven, 1954.

The Pelican Shakespeare. Edited by Alfred Harbage and Others. 38 vols. Baltimore, 1956-67.

Henry IV Part One. Edited by Maynard Mack. (The Signet Classic Shakespeare.) New York, 1965.

The New Penguin Shakespeare. Edited by T. J. B. Spencer, Stanley Wells, and Others. Harmondsworth, 1967 — (In progress.)

The First Folio of Shakespeare: The Norton Facsimile. Prepared by Charlton Hinman. New York, 1968.

Hamlet, Henry IV Part One, Julius Caesar, Macbeth. Edited by Maynard Mack and Robert W. Boynton. (The Hayden Shakespeare Series.) 4 vols. New York, 1973.

The Riverside Shakespeare. Edited by G. Blakemore Evans and Others. Boston, 1974.

Coriolanus. Edited by J. Philip Brockbank. (The Arden Shakespeare.) London, 1976.

B. Other Books and Articles

Alexander, Peter. "Restoring Shakespeare: The Modern Editor's Task," *Shakespeare Survey 5* (1952), pp. 1-9.

———. *Shakespeare's "Henry VI" and Richard III".* Cambridge, 1929.

Bernard, John. *Retrospections of the Stage.* 2 vols. London, 1830.

Butt, John. *Pope's Taste in Shakespeare.* (Shakespeare Association.) London, 1936.

Capell, Edward. *Notes and Various Readings to Shakespeare. Part the First.* London, 1774.

Chambers, E. K. *William Shakespeare: A Study of Facts and Problems.* 2 vols. Oxford, 1930.

Chetwood, William Rufus. *The British Theatre.* Dublin, 1750.

Flatter, Richard. *Shakespeare's Producing Hand.* London, 1948.

Fletcher, John. *Demetrius and Enanthe . . . Published from a Manuscript Dated 1625.* Edited by Alexander Dyce. London, 1830.

Greg, W. W. "The Bibliographical History of the First Folio," *The Library,* 2nd series, vol. IV no. 15 (July 1903), pp. 258-85.

———. *Dramatic Documents from the Elizabethan Playhouses.* 2 vols. Oxford, 1931.

———. *The Shakespeare First Folio: Its Bibliographical and Textual History.* Oxford, 1955.

———. *Two Elizabethan Stage Abridgements: "The Battle of Alcazar" & "Orlando Furioso".* (Malone Society.) Oxford, 1922.

Harrison, G. B. "A Note on *Coriolanus,*" *Joseph Quincy Adams Memorial Studies,* ed. James G. McManaway and

Others (Washington, 1948), pp. 239-52.

Honigmann, E. A. J. *The Stability of Shakespeare's Text.* London, 1965.

Johnson, Samuel. *Proposals for Printing . . . the Dramatick Works of William Shakespeare.* London, 1756.

Lee, Sidney. *A Life of William Shakespeare.* London, 1898.

Malone, Edmond. *A Dissertation on the Three Parts of King Henry VI.* London, 1787.

Marlowe, Christopher. *"Dido Queen of Carthage" and "The Massacre at Paris".* Edited by H. J. Oliver. London, 1968.

Marston, John. *The Fawn.* Edited by Gerald A. Smith. Lincoln (Nebraska), 1965.

Massinger, Philip. *Believe as You List.* Edited by T. Crofton Croker. (Percy Society, vol. 27.) London, 1849.

———. ———. Edited by Charles J. Sisson. (Malone Society.) Oxford, 1927.

McManaway, James G. "The Year's Contribution to Shakespearian . . . Textual Studies," *Shakespeare Survey 2* (1949), pp. 145-53.

Middleton, Thomas. *A Tragi-Coomodie called The Witch, long since acted by His Majesties Servants at the Black-Friers.* Edited by Isaac Reed. London, 1778.

Pollard, Alfred W. *Shakespeare's Fight with the Pirates and the Problems of the Transmission of his Text.* Cambridge, 1920.

———. W. W. Greg, E. Maunde Thompson, J. Dover Wilson, and R. W. Chambers. *Shakespeare's Hand in the*

Play of Sir Thomas More. Cambridge, 1923.

Sheridan, Richard Brinsley. *The Plays & Poems.* Edited by R. Crompton Rhodes. 2 vols. Oxford, 1928.

———. *The Dramatic Works.* Edited by Cecil Price. 2 vols. Oxford, 1973.

Smith, David Nichol. *Shakespeare in the Eighteenth Century.* Oxford, 1928.

Spevack, Marvin. *The Harvard Concordance to Shakespeare.* Cambridge (Massachusetts), 1973.

Theobald, Lewis. *Shakespeare Restored: or, a Specimen of the many errors, as well committed, as unamended, by Mr. Pope in his late edition of this poet.* London, 1726.

Thompson, Edward Maunde. *Shakespeare's Handwriting.* Oxford, 1916.

Warner, George F. "An Autograph Play of Philip Massinger," *The Athenaeum,* 19 January 1901, pp. 90-91.

Wilson, F. P. "Shakespeare and the 'New Bibliography'," *The Bibliographical Society 1892-1942: Studies in Retrospect* (London, 1949), pp. 76-135.

Wilkinson, Tate. *Memoirs of His Own Life.* 4 vols. York, 1790.

INDEX

Alexander, Peter, 42,44,52
Alleyn, Edward, 43
Bellott, Stephen, 51
Bentley, Richard, 22
Bernard, John, 42-3
Betterton, Thomas, 10,17
Boswell, James, the younger, 29,36
Boynton, Robert W., 65
Brockbank, J. Philip, 66-7
Bunbury, Sir Henry, 41
Burbage, Richard, 5
Butt, John, 21
Capell, Edward,
   13,15,17,24-7,29-30,36,38-9,45-6,51,60,71
Chambers, E. K., 29
Chambers, R. W., 51
Chettle, Henry, 47
Chetwind, Philip, 10,12,17
Chetwood, W. R., 49
Cibber, Colley, 49
Clark, William George, 30-1,36-41,67
Coleridge, Samuel Taylor, 18
Collier, John Payne, 41
Condell, Henry, 5-7,15-6,20,38-40,45,54,64
Cotes, Thomas, 7,10
Crane, Ralph, 47
Croker, T. Crofton, 49-50
Dekker, Thomas, 47
Dyce, Alexander, 46-7
Ervin, Sam, 19
Evans, G. Blakemore, 51,63
Fenton, Elijah, 15
Fitzgerald, F. Scott, 52
Flatter, Richard, 58,61
Fletcher, John, 7,28,46
Furnivall, Frederick J., 41
Gay, John, 15
Glover, John, 30-1,36-41,67
Granville-Barker, Harley, 55,71
Greene, Robert, 43
Greg, W. W., 44,48,50-1,53-4
Hanmer, Sir Thomas, 3,13-4,17,24,26,70
Harbage, Alfred, 62
Harrison, G. B., 55-8,61-3,65,68
Hemmings, John, 5-7,15-6,20,38-40,45,54,64
Henslowe, Philip, 43,48
Herbert, Sir Henry, 49
Heywood, Thomas 47
Honigmann, E. A. J., 54
Jaggard, William, 6-7

Johnson, Samuel,
   13-4,17,24,26-7,29,36-7,46,76-7
Jonson, Ben, 5
Knight, Charles, 38
Lee, Sidney, 47-8
Mack, Maynard, 62,65
Malone, Edmond,
   13-4,17,26-9,36-9,42,49
Marlowe, Christopher, 45
Marston, John, 71-2
Massinger, Philip, 49
McManaway, James G., 58,61
Middleton, Thomas, 46
Mountjoy, Christopher, 51
Munday, Anthony, 47
Oliver, H. J., 45
Pavier, Thomas, 5-6,10,16
Pollard, Alfred W., 5,41,44-5,48,51
Pope, Alexander,
   12-26,29,30,37-9,46,51,57,60,62,66-8,
   70,76-7
Price, Cecil, 42
Reed, Isaac, 27,29,46
Rhodes, R. Crompton, 42,44
Ridley, M. R., 61
Rowe, Nicholas,
   3,11-2,14-5,17,21-2,25,30,51,54-6,
   64,66
Sheridan, Richard Brinsley, 42-3
Simpson, Richard, 50
Sisson, Charles J., 49
Smith, Adam, 27
Smith, D. Nichol, 20
Smith, Gerald A., 72
Steevens, George,
   13,17,27-30,36,42,51,60,65-6,68,70
Theobald, Lewis, 13,17,22-4,26,30,51
Thiselton, Alfred Edward, 53
Thompson, Edward Maunde, 51-2
Tilney, Edmund, 47
Tonson, Jacob, 11-2,14-5,23
Waith, Eugene M., 61
Wallace, C. W., 51
Warburton, William, 13,17,24,26
Warner, Sir George, 49
Wilkinson, Tate, 42
Wilson, F. P., 47-8
Wilson, J. Dover, 51
Wright, William Aldis, 31,36-41,64,67